Gertrude Parsons

Afternoons with Mrs. Maitland

Gertrude Parsons

Afternoons with Mrs. Maitland

ISBN/EAN: 9783741178023

Manufactured in Europe, USA, Canada, Australia, Japa

Cover: Foto ©Andreas Hilbeck / pixelio.de

Manufactured and distributed by brebook publishing software (www.brebook.com)

Gertrude Parsons

Afternoons with Mrs. Maitland

AFTERNOONS

WITH

MRS. MAITLAND:

A

Book of Household Instruction and Entertainment.

BY

THE AUTHOR OF "EMMA'S CROSS," &c.

LONDON:
BURNS AND LAMBERT, 17 PORTMAN STREET,
AND 63 PATERNOSTER ROW.

CONTENTS.

CHAP.		PAGE
	INTRODUCTION	1
I.	TRUTH	7
II.	GENEROSITY	18
III.	DILIGENCE	29
IV.	KINDNESS	40
V.	DRESS	65
VI.	GOSSIP	78
VII.	CURIOSITY	91
VIII.	COURAGE, PRESENCE OF MIND, AND RECOLLECTION	105
IX.	MODESTY	123
X.	TEMPERANCE AND SOBRIETY	131
XI.	REVERENCE	142
XII.	CARELESSNESS	149
XIII.	GOOD MANAGEMENT	160
XIV.	JUSTICE	176
XV.	OBSERVATION	183
XVI.	OBEDIENCE	191

A

HOUSEHOLD BOOK

OF

INSTRUCTION AND ENTERTAINMENT.

INTRODUCTION.

THERE was in a large town a school for girls, which was attached to a convent. There were girls of various ages in this school, and they were divided into classes. It is of the first-class girls that I am going to tell you. Their ages were from ten years to seventeen. The girls of seventeen were quite young women, both in appearance and knowledge, though they were still considered as belonging to the school. The girls who were of this first class were treated differently from those of the other classes. They were allowed a large part of every day for doing various sorts of work, and for this they were paid; so that some of the cleverest and the most industrious could earn four or five shillings a week, and have the advantage of education and religious instruction besides. Some of them also were allowed to learn other things; they were sent to work in the kitchen of the servants' home, which was attached to the convent, and to do washing and ironing sometimes, and also housework occasionally. By these means they were fitted to become good intelligent servants; and at the time of which I am speaking, three of these first-class girls had got places, and they were to go, in about a month, to some distance from this school, where they had been from children, and from these nuns, who had been their best and kindest earthly friends.

These girls were called Mary Hardy, Anne Wilton, and Jane Isles. They were three good girls, and clever girls too; and they were very glad to get into respectable places, though they did look sorrowful sometimes, and had to wipe their eyes over the nice clothes they were now busily making to take to their new homes.

Several ladies were in the habit of visiting this school, and the girls were very glad to see them. The first-class girls had most to do with these ladies, for the ladies had taken the responsibility of getting them work; and they got orders for collars and trimmings; and brought many things with them for these girls to do; and they often prepared the work, and showed them the best way of doing it; and so the ladies were always very welcome, and they were always very kind. A subscription had been made to reward these girls who were going to leave the school, among these friends of theirs; and materials had been purchased enough to make a respectable quantity of clothes for each of them. One of the ladies—perhaps she was the one the girls liked best, though they could hardly have told why—had undertaken to cut out all their clothes, and to bring her maid, who was a good dressmaker, to make the gowns fit properly, and trim the bonnets, and make up the new caps. All the linen she undertook to cut out herself; and she said she should like to talk to them while they worked, and hear their questions about the lives they were likely to lead, and give them any information that she could. This was consented to; and as the workroom was separated from the schoolroom, it was arranged that every afternoon the first-class girls should meet, and work under this lady's instructions, and think over the subjects that might be most closely connected with their future interests in life.

"Mary Hardy," said Mrs. Maitland, "why is that apron you are making so much larger than all your others?"

"I have three large aprons, ma'am," said Mary; "I am going to be under-housemaid, and these are the aprons in which I shall do my morning's work. If you please, ma'am, you said, that if I had not some large aprons, I should dirty the counterpane and valances when I made the beds; because I can have clean aprons oftener than I can have clean gowns."

"Very well," said the lady.

"Are you all making aprons?" was the next question; and all three girls said,

"Yes, ma'am."

"Yours look very coarse, Anne Wilton."

"Yes, ma'am; I am the kitchen-maid. These canvas-aprons are to scour the saucepans and scrub the stone floors in."

"And yours, Jane Isles?"

"Mine are parlour-maid's aprons. They have nice

pockets; that is to hold the little dusters I shall dust the china-ornaments with."

"Why *little* dusters?" asked Mrs. Maitland.

"Large dusters do for furniture, but little dusters are best for delicate things. I might sweep ornaments off their stands with the ends of large dusters, the housekeeper told me."

"Do you think you shall like your places?"

"O yes," said each of the girls.

"Of course you expect trials?"

"Yes," said Mary Hardy, very gravely.

"There are trials every where," said Anne Wilton, with a smile.

"I don't know," said Jane Isles.

"But," said Mary, speaking again, "we were saying, as we walked home last night, that we wished you, ma'am, would tell us something of the tempers and dispositions expected of us in the new lives that we are going to lead; and also something of the best way of doing our duty to our souls, as well as towards our fellow-servants and our employers. We shall think of school, and love the time we have spent here. But we should like to mix up the thoughts of service with our last thoughts of this place; and will you help us to do this, Mrs. Maitland? We asked Sister Angela if we might ask you, and she said it was a good thought of ours, if you would comply with it. Will you, dear ma'am? We should all of us thank you."

So the consequence of this request was, that Mrs. Maitland began to tell the girls, as they sat at work, of their future trials and temptations; and of the lives that, as good and well-instructed Catholics, they ought to lead. And the first virtue she spoke of, and how she spoke of it, you will see in the following chapter.

Of course all the girls in the workroom listened; but the three girls who were to go to their places, and begin to take care of themselves in the world so soon, listened with greater interest than any others. They sat nearest to Mrs. Maitland; and they sometimes dropped their work on their knees to listen as she talked. Recollections also came to their minds when she asked questions, or in any way appealed to their hearts and judgments; and now and then they accused themselves secretly of not having always acted as she said all good Catholics should act; and when she explained why Catholics in the world should be careful to persevere strictly in all virtue, because the honour of the Church of God was in their hands, as well as the safety of their souls, then they determined to adorn their situations in life with all their powers; not going through life negligently, and doing as little as possible, but always doing their best with head and hand and heart, because the all-seeing eye of God beholds them, and His mercy offers grace, and His goodness gives power; and because His love has its accomplishment in those who are GOOD.

So Mrs. Maitland,—having asked with a smile, "Are you all going to listen?" and having had "Yes, yes, yes," in answer,—said,

"You must remember that I am not going to teach you your religion,—you all know that. I am not going to tell you that you must be honest and pure,—you know that. I am going to give you such instructions as occur to a woman who, like myself, has lived a great many years in the world. You are beginning the world for yourselves. You have, up to this time, been *helped* to live properly—been guided by friends. Now you are not going to be helped in this way any longer. Your own hearts and consciences must guide you, and you will perhaps very soon be called to give to others that friendly help which others have given to you. And so, to help you to know yourselves, and to understand what the Church expects of you, and to warn you of some of the troubles and difficulties that may be thrown in your way, I am going to give you the benefit of a little of my own experience. And I shall often think with pleasure, my dear girls," said Mrs. Maitland, "that you have asked for some last words from me to take away in your memory, to help you in the world. And now we will first think and talk about—TRUTH."

What was said about truth, and many other virtues, and some faults, is now offered to you, dear readers, in a printed book, for your pleasure and instruction, if you will read and remember it.

CHAPTER I.

TRUTH.

You know that the devil is the father of lies. The first lie that ever was told upon earth was told by the devil when he tempted Eve in Paradise, and said that they should not surely die if they disobeyed Almighty God. Whoever tells lies copies the devil.

But Almighty God is Eternal Truth. Upon His truth we depend, and His truth we adore all our lives. Whoever tells truth bravely, constantly, and religiously, copies God, follows the example of our Lord Jesus Christ, and behaves uprightly, as all ought to behave who belong to Jesus and live by the Sacraments.

Throughout all nations and countries truth is honoured, and falsehood despised. An old poet, called George Herbert, says,

"Dare to be true; nothing can need a lie;
The fault that needs it most grows two thereby."

You can easily remember this rhyme, and you may often repeat it to yourself, for there is wisdom and truth in it.

"*Dare* to be true," said the poet. Yes, dare! for it sometimes requires great courage, and you have to *dare to* be true; and if you don't dare, then you are a coward, and cowards tell lies. Think what daring the first Christians showed who heard Mass and received the Sacraments in places underground, called the Catacombs, in Rome. They were not foolishly or wrongly careless of life; for life is God's gift, and we are not to throw it away carelessly. They did not court danger; but when danger came, when it was discovered that they were Christians, and they were asked the question, then they told the truth. They would not tell a lie even to save their lives.

They used to be put into a large open space surrounded by galleries, where the Roman pagans were assembled; and terrible beasts—lions or tigers or panthers—were ready to rush out and tear them to pieces.

One lie would have saved them from this awful death; but they would not tell it. Only just for that once to tell a lie and pretend they were not Christians would have saved them; but truth was dearer than life. They would not dishonour our Blessed Lord by telling a lie and denying Him, even for a single hour. And so the wild-beasts rushed at them; and helpless young girls felt the horrible fangs of the hungry animals, and fell on the sand torn and dead. Such truth won the crown of martyrdom. There are but few of the noble army of martyrs who could not have saved their lives if they had chosen to tell a lie. Thinking of them should make you feel firm and strong on the side of truth.

For the honour of God you must tell the truth, for lying lips are an abomination to God. We are told by God in the Holy Scriptures that He hates liars. You must also tell the truth for the love of God's holy Church, to which you belong, and which has not left you ignorant of your duty. It is quite certain, as holy priests tell you, that if you could take every soul out of purgatory by telling a lie, you must not tell it. As is said in the rhyme I have quoted to you, "nothing can need a lie."

Then, again, it is so foolish to tell a lie; it is so silly not to be true. You can't mend a fault by denying it, or excusing it with a lie. You must see quite plainly that to tell a lie to hide a fault is doing a second bad action, when before you had done but one. Then, if you have not committed a sin, but only done something that is not very wise, and if to hide or excuse this you say what is not true,—what then?. Why, you have stained your soul with a sin just to hide some small error. Is that wise? It is not wise, and it is not right. We must never tell a lie. If any of us are ever so overcome as to depart from truth, we must beg God's pardon, and ask for grace and strength never to fall in that way again; and, having repented and made good resolutions, we must take that sin to confession.

Many people will acknowledge, that to take a falsehood to confession is a great act of humiliation. Many people acknowledge that they have experienced a great difficulty in confessing this sin. The devil knows this very well. He likes to tempt people away from the truth. If he can only make them careless about truth, and accustom them to falsehood, he knows that he shall get their poor souls into his grasp at last, unless—using that power that every Catholic has till he throws it away by persevering in sin—unless they rise up bravely and accuse themselves before God, and get forgiven and cleansed, and made strong in the blessed Sacrament of

Penance. Thus, you see, the old poet was wise when he said in his rhyme, "*Dare* to be true." You must, indeed, be courageous about this. If you encourage a spirit of falsehood, you put your soul in great danger.

Consider, now, as a Catholic, how dangerous it is to depart from truth. We know very well that falsehood brings us at last into that state that we deceive ourselves. A Catholic, so deceived, might make bad confessions. This thought alone should make us value truth beyond all calculation.

We know that when a Catholic goes to confession his soul should be like an open book spread out before God. Every fault, just as it was committed, in its own truth, should be told simply. This is easiest to those persons who are always truthful, who venerate truth and practise it in daily life, and in all their words and works. "Lord, who shall dwell in Thy tabernacle, or who shall rest on Thy holy hill?" These words Almighty God put into King David's mouth, and He also gave us the answer: "He that speaketh truth in his heart, who hath not used deceit in his tongue."

But perhaps some people feel that it is very difficult to tell truth always. People ask questions that we don't want to answer; and they sometimes press for an answer in such a way, that we are tempted to tell an untruth to stop them. Here, again, we must show courage. If people ask impertinent questions, we can refuse to answer them; and we *must* refuse to answer rather than tell a falsehood. Perhaps you have heard this saying, "Truth is not to be spoken at all times." Ignorant people think that the meaning of this is, that sometimes they may tell a lie. Foolish and ignorant as this is, there are people who think so. The readers of these pages have been better taught; they know that the real meaning of that saying is, that people are sometimes so placed that they must not tell what they know,—not speak at all perhaps, or even refuse plainly to give an answer to the question asked. This little story will explain how this may be.

One day two young girls stood by the door of a farmhouse. There had been a quarrel between two of the farm-boys. The elder girl knew all about this quarrel; the younger girl did not know the particulars. She only knew that the quarrel was about a hen's nest that had been robbed, and that a small boy called Charlie Bennet had mentioned the name of another boy whom he had seen at a suspiciously late hour in the yard. While they were standing at the house-door, they saw Charlie Bennet run through the meadow below the house as fast as he could go. They did not see which way he took when he had left the meadow. About five minutes after, a boy, much bigger than Charlie, called Jem Jones, stopped at the door quite out of breath with running, and looking very red in the face.

"Where is Charlie Bennet?" he asked of the elder girl.

"I don't know," she said; and she said no more.

"Oh," said the younger girl, "he ran through the meadow a few minutes ago. He went to the right hand; under the elm-trees I saw him last."

On went Jem Jones towards the elm-trees as fast as he could run.

"O Kitty," said the elder girl, "you ought not to have said that."

"Why not?" said Kitty; "it was the truth. There can't be any harm in telling the truth."

"The truth is not to be spoken at all times," answered the elder girl, whose name was Anne.

"Do you mean that I ought to have told a lie?" said Kitty very loud, and looking angry.

"No," said Anne, "that is not my meaning. You ought not to have said any thing; you know the boys have been quarrelling. You were not obliged to speak; and you ought not to have spoken."

"Well, then," said Kitty, "why did not you say that we had seen Charlie?"

"Because I was not asked if we had seen him. I saw Jem was hot, and I thought he was angry. It was Jem's brother that Charlie mentioned as having been by the hen-roost last night."

It was just as Anne feared. Jem ran after Charlie, caught him, and beat him in his anger so badly, that Charlie was made very ill, and had a fever; and when he was at the worst, Jem's brother went to the farmer, and confessed that he really had taken the eggs, and that poor little Charlie had only told the truth to his master. Then Jem Jones was very sorry for having behaved so cruelly to Charlie; and being a very passionate boy, he got angry with Kitty, and told her it was all her fault. Why had she told him where Charlie had been seen last? it was she who put him on the way to find him. If she had not done that, Charlie would never have suffered. It was all her fault.

And so it got about that it was all Kitty's fault,—every body said it was Kitty's fault. It was of no use to deny it; if Kitty said that the fault was Jem's, Jem answered,

"Why did you tell me where to go? Why did you tell me where to find him?"

So at last Kitty gave up disputing about it; but she always remembered this in her heart,—that there are times when you are not obliged to tell what you know, and when it is wisest and best to say nothing; and this is the true meaning of the saying, that the truth is not to be spoken at all times.

You see that, in this instance, Kitty was not obliged to speak at all; but if you are obliged to speak, then you are *never*, neither for hope of gain nor fear of loss, to hide the truth, or even to cloud it over and make it obscure or doubtful. When you are obliged to speak, or when your judgment tells you that it is right to speak, then speak out plainly. Tell what you know simply and truly, without deceit or reservation. You will find, as you go through life, that occasions will arise when it will be your duty as a good Catholic to tell the truth, even when you are not asked to do so. Sometimes it may be due to your own character to do so; often it may be your duty towards your neighbour to speak; for instances frequently occur when troubles and hard thoughts and trying suspicions are all cleared away by one right-minded person telling the simple truth in the right manner and at the proper time. When we have the opportunity of doing such a good action, we should never hesitate, but go and do it bravely, simply, and kindly, for the good of our neighbour and for the love of God.

As we go through life, we should, for the love of truth, be careful about our promises. Don't make promises lightly; and don't break a promise, unless you have a just cause for doing so. If you break a promise, take the first opportunity of explaining why it was, in order that you may not be supposed guilty of disregarding your word.

We must detest and despise falsehood, and we must love and respect truth. We must not encourage any deceit in our hearts, or practise any falsehood or deceit with our tongue. And we must be careful never to encourage falsehood or deceit in others. You must remember this in dealing with children particularly. When a child tells a lie, it is often from fright. We may not have been unkind to a child to produce this fright. Perhaps children have naturally a sort of fear of those who are so much bigger and stronger than themselves, and who exercise entire power over them.

Children, with their pure innocent minds, know when they have done wrong much more quickly than many people think, and feel more about it than thoughtless people believe. All really good, observing, religious nurses tell us so. Remember this; and, as you may have the care of children one day, be most particular to preserve a child's sincerity and truth; and never teach it how to deceive by accusations, and that sort of cross-examination which would fret and displease a grown-up person, and is a dangerous trial to a child. Very good people often tease children in this way, and do them a real injury without even intending to do any thing but good. An example will explain what is meant very easily.

You see that a little child just able to speak has done wrong. *You* know it, and the child knows it too. Now a foolish mother or nurse will begin with questions. "Have you done that? Were you so naughty? Tell me; did you do it? What! won't you speak?" All this time, this little tender child is frightened and ashamed, and of course getting vexed at being asked so many questions, and being proved guilty so many times. Shame and fear and annoyance prevent her speaking. But the silly woman has told her to speak; and she must speak, even if her full little heart feels bursting, because she has been told to speak; or if she won't, or perhaps can't, she is accused of a new fault, and called disobedient, and, perhaps, sulky and ill-tempered, and obstinate, and not at all sorry. Every one of these accusations that child feels is a falsehood. She is not wise enough yet to dispute the point, but she *feels it in her heart* just as truly as if she was ten years old. Then she begins to vindicate herself, and to deny every thing. "I didn't, I didn't!" she says; and the foolish mother or nurse says, "You did; you know you did!" So, in this way, before a child is two years old, there may be quarrels about truth.

Once, just what I have described happened. It was a lady, the child's mother, who was so foolish. An upper-servant passing by, entered the nursery, and having been a nurse herself all through her early life, she understood in an instant what the trouble was about.

The good woman took the child up in her arms, and mentioned its fault plainly. "Missey made a hammer of her doll, and broke the pretty little picture." The child sobbed out, "Yes; broke the glass." "Missey mustn't break any more pictures; missey must tell mamma that she won't break any more: and she is very sorry, isn't she?" So the mother held out her arms, and the child dropped into them, and said she was sorry, and fell asleep in five minutes.

Then the mother said to the old servant, "O Mary, I wish I could manage children as you do."

"Please, ma'am, never set up a child's temper, never let a child begin contradicting. If a child learns 'You did!' and 'I didn't!' so early in life, it will never accept truth as a child ought to accept it. And besides that, I am always afraid of frightening or worrying a child into telling falsehoods. One never knows what a dispute may end in. And if little children are worried into lying, any thing else may follow; they may grow up to be false throughout." So spoke this good woman, who encouraged truth, even in a very little child, as a bright virtue; knowing that without it no character can be long respected, and knowing also, that to grow accustomed to falsehood, is to live on familiar terms with the father of all falsehoods,—the devil.

A holy priest taught this prayer to those who came to him: "O SPIRIT OF TRUTH, who lovest truth, make me also to love it." We cannot do better than say this prayer ourselves.

Here Mrs. Maitland stopped. It was time for the

girls to go home. "Thank you, thank you, Mrs. Maitland," was said several times. And then as they walked home the girls said, "O truth, precious truth! Truth seems to make every thing easy."

"Oh, yes," said Mary Hardy; "with truth in our own hearts, and with truth in the hearts of all around us, how easy it would be to go through life!—like walking on a fine free road without a stone or a pitfall in it. The trials of life seem oftenest to arise from falsity,— some deceitful action, some false word, even false smiles and treacherous kindness. I hope I shall find friends full of truth. I will not mind blame, or quickness of temper, or any such trials; I think I could bear any thing if I should still find truth in other people's hearts, and by God's grace keep it in my own."

And then they all said the prayer of the holy priest: "O Spirit of Truth, who lovest truth, make me also to love it."

CHAPTER II.

GENEROSITY.

"WE will talk to-day about Generosity," said Mrs. Maitland. Generosity does not mean giving away money only. Generous-minded people do give money where money is wanted, and, if they have it to give, with great willingness, making people welcome to all the help they can afford very heartily. But generous-minded people give every day and every hour other things that are even better than money sometimes,—they give kind judgments. Even when appearances are so much against a person, that it is almost impossible not to believe the person guilty of the fault of which they are accused,—even when other people, and good people, condemn,—the generous-minded will hope, will not believe altogether what others believe; and, at last, will find a great many excuses for the accused person. It is a very happy thing to know that the generous-minded person is very often right; that people are often accused of wilful faults, when they have only made mistakes; and that people have been found to be perfectly innocent of grave crimes, even when very learned and wise persons have condemned them as guilty. Always, then, encourage generous feelings in your mind; always hope the best for people; and always do all in your power to help and comfort the friends and neighbours among whom God has placed you.

There are some whom it is your duty to help; your parents, for instance. They come first. You are never to be ashamed of them. Suppose they are very low in the world; suppose they are supported by the parish—perhaps in the poor-house. You may send them such help as you can; but if you keep away from them from shame, you do very wrong, and are ungenerous, even if you give them half of what you earn.

Your love should always wait upon them. You should show them even more attention than is theirs by right, if there is any difference between your station and theirs,—if they have fallen, and you have risen, in the world. This is a sort of generosity that pleases God; for in our duties, as well as in our alms, God loveth a cheerful giver. There is a true story of a generous youth which will please you very much if you are generous-minded yourself. You know that there are such things in England as ragged-schools. Well, there have long been ragged-schools in Rome; though there is no poverty in any Catholic country such as we see in England, and no rags and starvation in Rome like the rags and starvation in London and other great towns in this country. These Roman ragged-schools are held in the evening after work-hours; so the poor boys earn what they can, and then learn all they are able to learn in the hours that are left before night comes. The Holy Father, our beloved Pope Pius IX., loves these schools, and sometimes himself gives the prizes with his own hand, and speaks holy words of love and encouragement to the boys. You will say that this is very generous-minded of the Holy Father; and so it is. He knows that this offering from his own great heart will make their young hearts glad, and so he will not deny to these boys what will give them pleasure and strength.

Every Easter the children are examined in their catechism publicly in a church, where many of the cardinals and persons of rank and dignity go to hear them. Prizes are given, and the boy who gets the first place is called the Emperor. The emperor is then taken to the Pope, and the Pope blesses him, and tells him to ask for something, and his request is given to him. This is a great privilege. Some boys, as you may suppose, like to be placed out in some trade, in which they hope to succeed; some, who are fond of learning, may, perhaps, ask to be educated in some particular school, by which they may become learned men in time. Every "emperor" has some hope for himself, and the fulfilment of this is what he thinks of, when he asks his favour of the Pope.

A few years ago, a boy of about fourteen was very good at school, and most diligent in his studies. He worked about in the day wherever he could get a job, and came regularly to school in the evenings. This boy had a bad father; but he was very good himself. The father committed a great crime; which was found out, and he was tried, and condemned to death. It must have been hard for the boy to keep good, with the shadow upon him of his father's deep sin and dark disgrace. But he did keep good, and *very* good too: no boy in Rome was more honest in his daily work, and no scholar in the school was more diligent in his learning. In fact, he knew that every thing depended on himself. His father would be executed; and he had no friends but those that he made by his own good conduct. You will not be surprised to hear that this boy had made up his mind to be emperor that year.

The day of the examination came; and all the children were assembled in the church, and all the great people were there to hear them. I don't think that this boy felt frightened, for he had prayed every day that he might succeed. He had prayed in the proper way; so earnestly that you would have thought every thing depended on those prayers alone, and yet working as diligently as if every thing depended on himself; so, with this right and proper union of faith and works, I don't think he felt much afraid. If another boy won, it would be the will of God that it should be so, and he intended to submit to the will of God, and even to accept and love it, whatever it might be; and if he won,—oh, if he won, he knew what he should ask of the Pope! He did win. When the examination was over, there stood this boy emperor. Now what is he going to ask of the Pope, this poor friendless boy, whose father is a bad father, and who stands by himself in the world? If he asks to be placed in the army or the navy, it will be granted. If he asks to be made a tradesman or a farmer, it will be done. He kneels, and asks for his father's life. The holy Pope, with tears in his eyes, blesses him; and the criminal is released from prison, and given up to this good boy.

This was doing more than filial duty strictly demanded of him. It is a great instance not only of a child's duty to a parent, but of generous-mindedness.

Now always try to do more than you are obliged to do. Don't weigh and measure your duties, but be generous, generous to the utmost of your abilities; form generous habits: you will receive as much pleasure as you give.

This is not asking you to be over-indulgent, to encourage people in bad habits, to take other people's duties on yourself, so as to spoil their characters, and do them harm instead of good. If you have common sense and judgment, which a Catholic education has formed and instructed, you will clearly see the difference between being generous-minded and weakly indulgent.

For instance, if a fellow-servant, through illness, was sleepy in the mornings, and feeling worn with a bad night, it would be generous to get up earlier yourself, and do some of her work, not once or twice, but many times. But if a young girl was lazy, or overslept herself, because she would not try to break herself of a bad habit, then you might do her work once or twice from a generous feeling towards your master and mistress, that they might not suffer inconvenience from a foolish girl's bad conduct; but you would do no kindness to this girl by continuing to do her work, you would only be over-indulgent.

It is the misfortune of uneducated girls not to see distinctions; but those who read this book will not, it is hoped, be of this class. You can fancy an uneducated good girl thinking she would be very generous-minded, and, from never having had her judgment properly strengthened and instructed, doing all sorts of absurd things, and being very troublesome and mischievous. Such a girl was once engaged as parlour-maid. She got up very early one morning, and she thought she would be generous to the cook, so she lighted the kitchen fire. Of course, when cook came down she laughed and was well pleased. Then she had ten minutes to spare, and she cleaned the knives left from supper, which pleased the scullery-maid very much. Then she ran up stairs about her own work, and put the jug of hot water at her mistress's door, and ran down again as fast as she could to lay the parlour breakfast. She was very merry, and in a very good temper, and had worked as fast as the cleverest girl in the world.

When she takes away breakfast her mistress says very gravely, "You are a new servant, and I wish to tell you a few things. Your master, who is, as you know, a great invalid, had a bad night, and he could have slept this morning, only you have such a habit of running on the stairs, and that kept him awake; this annoyed me very much. When I took my hot-water jug this morning, I found brick-dust about the handle, and something black. I am sorry to say that some of this black got upon my sleeves; and as they match my collar, and I am going out this morning, Ellen will have to wash them in a hurry. I also see some of this same black on the table-cloth. Perhaps it may stain it. Tell the scullery-maid to go with it to the washerwoman this morning. And ask cook to step here;

we shall not dine early with the children; as your master was disturbed this morning, we will dine later by ourselves."

Though the lady spoke rather gravely, the girl did not think such trifles worth troubling about. She gave the messages, and went up stairs to her work in the bedrooms. But by the servants' dinner-time, she found that every one in the house was cross, and cross with her.

"Look here, now," said Kate the scullery-maid, "I would rather clean the knives than have such a hot walk as I have had to-day to the washerwoman with the parlour-cloth that you stained with the black-lead, with which you cleaned cook's fireplace. I'm just killed," said Kate, angrily. "You do *your* work, and I'll do *mine*."

The cook spoke next.

"Yes," she said, "and very ill could I spare you, having myself an extra dinner to dress, because poor master was disturbed this morning; why you must have run up and down stairs like a young colt."

The young woman felt very angry, but before she could speak, Ellen came in with her mistress's sleeves, just washed, in her hand.

"Here," she said, "make room before the fire. I want to dry these sleeves. Such a trouble! and I was so busy this morning. How could you be such a busybody, dirtying your hands with doing other people's work! You have got every body into trouble."

The girl went away into her own little pantry, and there cried heartily. But she was very angry.

"I'll never do another kind thing while I live in this house," she said to herself. "I *will* do my own work in future, and nothing else,—nothing else! they have had the last piece of kindness from me." Of course you see that the girl was wrong.

A week or two after this, she saw Ellen coming down stairs with a tray full of things, which she had brought from her sick master's room. The scullery-maid had just finished scrubbing the stairs, and she had left a piece of soap on one of the steps.

"Don't step on the soap," said the young woman.

"Where is it? I can't see it," said Ellen; "move it away for me."

But she remembered what Ellen had said, and answered sharply, "I thought you told me not to dirty my hands with doing other people's work!"

At that moment Ellen stepped on the soap and fell violently forward, and lay quite insensible on the stone floor of the hall.

Sad and bitter were that girl's thoughts then. She knelt down and tried to recover the woman; but for many minutes she feared that she was dead. The whole household gathered round, and the poor sufferer was placed on a sofa, and a doctor sent for. She was a long time before she recovered her senses, and then she could not bear the light, and was sick; and it was more than a fortnight before she could go about by herself, and try to do part of her work. The young woman told the whole truth; and though every one blamed her, and at first her mistress wished to discharge her, yet, on her honest repentance, she was forgiven. And her mistress, having heard the whole story, tried to show her how different a true generosity of mind is from that busy way which probably only arises from a silly vanity, and a desire after praise.

This young woman became an excellent servant, and a good, steady, prudent, generous woman. Every one in the house felt that she was their friend, and that they had found a treasure in her.

Let it be so with you. Be generous from your heart, and you will be the benefactor of many. Do your own particular duties well, and try to live in love and kindness with all around. Cheerfully forgiving, mercifully helping people, generously thinking the best of your neighbours, thankfully accepting kindnesses, and gratefully returning them; always remembering how much our Blessed Lord has done for you, and always trying for His sake to do well and feel kindly towards every body. It is very easy to feel kind and generous on great occasions; but a good Catholic is generous about little things, and is kind always. Every day a great many opportunities arise for showing this good disposition. Remember that your life is made up of little things. Great miseries, and sorrow, and death, are not happening to *you* every day. But you can be generous in judging, generous in service, generous in patience, generous even in reproof and in prayer; for sometimes it may be your duty to reprove a friend, and you must always pray for your friends, both living and dead.

first they had all thought it would be a very dull conversation, for each girl said in her heart that *she* could never be generous: what had she to give? and certainly to be generous, meant to give something. But as their friend went on, each girl felt that she was richer than she had ever before imagined. And that evening, as they put on their cloaks, when Sister Angela said, "Have you been pleased this afternoon?"

Jane Isles answered with a merry smile, "Oh, yes, sister; we have found a fortune."

"A fortune!" exclaimed the nun.

"Yes, each one of us has found a fortune," said Anne Wilton; "Jane is right."

"And are all your fortunes the same? Are you all equally rich?" said the nun.

At this the girls looked at each other, and with thoughtful faces.

"I am the poorest," said Mary Hardy solemnly.

"Oh, I am too stingy and heartless to give properly," said Anne Wilton at the same time.

And Jane Isles said, "I could give, if I were not lazy."

"However, you all have the riches," said Sister Angela.

"Yes," answered Mary Hardy, "because God gives the power and the opportunity; and we let the power lie idle, and the opportunity pass by. That is what we mean by being poor, and stingy, and idle; we all, then, mean the same thing."

"But," said their friend, "you never before thought so much of your power, and of the riches that lie in

28 BOOK OF INSTRUCTION AND ENTERTAINMENT.

every Christian's heart. When you are out in the world, you will remember that you have something to give,—*much* to give, very often,—perhaps *more* to give than can ever be repaid you in this world. You will remember this. You will never let an opportunity pass by. You will be generous for the sake of the Cross,—for the love of God."

CHAPTER III.

DILIGENCE.

The next time that Mrs. Maitland and her young friends met, she told them that she thought they had better talk about Diligence.

"Oh, yes," said Anne Wilton, "we ought to understand that. We know something of diligence. When I look at the clock, and say to myself, I won't look up again from my work,—no, not for an instant,—unless I am positively obliged to look up, till the hour strikes, and when I really *do not* look up till I hear the first stroke, then I am diligent."

But little Jane Isles laughed. "Do you really ever do that?"

"Yes, very often," said Anne, rather proudly; "and I call that being diligent."

"I call it bondage and slavery," said Jane, smiling; "and I don't think that diligence can be bondage and slavery, for then it would be misery."

"Oh, help, Mary Hardy!" cried Anne; "we are getting into a great confusion."

"I suppose," said Mary, who was older than the other two, and a very thoughtful girl,—"I suppose that you are diligent when you work till the clock strikes without looking up; but you are diligent for a certain time only and for a certain purpose, just to find out how much you can do in a given time, and to amuse yourself. And I am sure you could not be diligent in that way all your life and about every thing you do, because it would be living in such an anxious state, and great anxieties are not good. I suppose that the diligence Mrs. Maitland will recommend will be a help, not a fatigue; something that will do us good, and not wear us out, as I am afraid you diligence would certainly do, if it could last long enough."

"I think you are right," said Anne.

"And to say so is generous and truthful too," said Jane, with her merry smile. "But here comes Mrs. Maitland; now listen."

"Are you ready?" asked the lady.

"Yes, ma'am; quite ready."

So Mrs. Maitland began: Diligence is the exact contrary to idleness. A diligent person masters her work, and does not let her work master her. Every body has something to do in this world, and unless they are diligent, they will seldom do it properly. A diligent person does not stand about in idleness for one half of a day, and then work hard the other half. But she does things with a settled determination, and with regularity and industry; not wasting time. Giving her mind to her work; so that one thing comes after another regularly and in proper succession, till the duty of the day is done, and the time that she may call her own is come.

Try with your might to be diligent. Diligence gives you that mastery over your work which it is right for a reasonable being to have, and which is a great comfort to a good Catholic. You are called by God to work; and to work is your duty. Learn, then, to work in such a way that you may do it without injury to your soul.

There are cases of people being so overloaded with business that they are hurried and pressed for time, and in a perpetual trouble at not being able to get the day's work done in the day. This is a great trial, and often, when this is the case, the employer is to blame. But a great many young women think themselves overloaded with work when it is not really the case.

If you find that you have engaged yourself to fulfil the duties of a very hard place, don't give up discontentedly; but try if, by diligence, you cannot master the work that is before you. Get up at a proper time, and keep to the practice diligently. Never neglect your prayers. They may be short; they must be said. Remember that. Be diligent with your work. Do it well, and as quickly as you can. Waste not one moment of time. Don't loiter over your meals. Don't cast things aside into wrong places, so as to oblige you to spend precious moments in looking for them the next day. Put every thing in its place. Order your work properly. Do first what will be first wanted. If you are called off from your work, never be cross. Think that it is part of your duty to bear these things,—and so bear them well and cheerfully, and get quickly back to your regular work, and by a little more diligence make up for having been called away from it. Get your work into regular order if possible. Do the same things one after another every day, if you can. This orderly way of going on will help you very much. Things get quicker done and better done if they are done in one way regularly every day. If your employer has not arranged all this for you, you must try to do it for yourself; and if you have learnt at school to use your senses and to judge properly, you will do this wisely and well after a little trial and experience. A busy life is not bad for the soul; that thought ought to comfort you. Doing your work diligently is, in fact, doing your duty all day long; and that is exactly what God requires of you. Thinking about your work does not mean that you are forgetting God. As a member of the Church of Christ, you ought never to forget God.

Take an example from many people who are leading very laborious lives in this country, earning their daily bread with unceasing diligence, and never forgetting God. Perhaps they are in a shop, lifting heavy weights, and measuring quantities for customers; standing all day, and giving constant and cheerful attention to one person after another from morning to night.

This is, in some cases, a very wearying life. But they do not forget God; they have had their passions under right control; they have kept their souls unpolluted in His sight; they have thought of Him often through the day; they have done many little acts of kindness to their neighbours for His sake. They have taken their meals with thankfulness, and made the sign of the Cross in the name of the blessed Trinity before and after them; they said their morning prayers at the beginning of the day, and they will not lie down till they have examined their consciences and recommended themselves to God with thanksgiving and faith. Many Catholics in this country are thus doing laborious work, and not forgetting God.

Hard work is never any excuse for forgetting God. God can be served *in* your work. They work best who work for God's sake, and with the feeling that, however hard their work is, they are fulfilling His adorable will. But the great thing to be avoided is, that hurry of mind, that confusion of thought, which seems to make it impossible to go on steadily and with a mind which is both peaceful and active at the same time. A great many very hard-working people are overpowered by the confusion that arises from having many things to do; but a young woman who has learnt how to be diligent at her work will have become orderly too. She will have learnt her work so well, and she will do it so steadily, that all feeling of hurry will pass away; she will work with both head and hands, and keep her self-possession, and her thoughts will not get into confusion; *she* will have no trouble in serving God in her work; *she* will soon be looked upon as an ornament to the Church, from whose teaching she has learnt what her duties are, and from whose Sacraments she has received strength to fulfil them.

You must, then, learn to be diligent for the sake of your soul.

Think of your soul as a precious jewel, which you possess and which lies in your breast, of which you have to take the greatest care, and which grows bright or dull as you do well or ill. Doing a great many things every day in an "any-how," confused, hurrying, disorderly way, is very likely to draw off your attention from this beautiful jewel; and then it will certainly grow dull, for you will not properly care about it. But doing a great many things every day, *and doing them all well*, will brighten this precious jewel; for every good action a Christian performs in a Christianlike way adds to the merit which shall surround that precious soul when its day of judgment comes. Learn, then, to be diligent for the sake of your soul, praising God in your work.

A great many people work very hard and with wonderful diligence, who have not been called by God to earn their living. You should think sometimes of how priests work for the love of Jesus, and in His great cause, for the salvation of souls. Such thoughts may be made very encouraging to people who feel that their places are hard, and that great exertions are required of them.

We have many priests in India with the army. You shall now have one day of their work described to you,—not the hardest day that can be picked out, but a day of the usual sort. See how diligent such a priest must be! During the heat of the day in summer in India, it is almost impossible for a person from this country to live without a large number of servants to take upon them all fatigue, and leave the poor Englishman as little to do as possible. These servants are the natives of the country, who are accustomed to the sun. Even in the night, during what is called the hottest season, it is so sultry that many persons could not sleep unless they were fanned all night; and where there is no machine for keeping the air in motion, two servants have to fan the sleeping person all night long. But generally there is a machine, whose motion keeps the air moving just as a fan moves it; and often water is thrown over this, so that the hot dry air is not only moved, but moistened and cooled by the motion of this thing, which is called a Punkah. But only the best accommodations are furnished with a punkah; and the Catholic priest of whom we are now to think has no punkah, and no servants to take it in turns to fan him; he lies down in the heat, and makes the best of it. If he sleeps, he thanks God; —perhaps we scarcely think of thanking God for sleep, unless we are ill;—if he lies awake, he tries to keep quiet, for he has work to do when day comes. A fly with a very irritating poisonous bite, the musquito, almost puts people into fevers when they first go to India, and are always a troublesome trial there. The priest hears this little insect singing in the air, and expects to have many red irritating lumps by morning; but he does not disturb himself. He has lizards in his room, and the lizards eat the musquitoes; and he knows that they will destroy those flies better than he can, and so he makes up his mind to be still. "Lizards in his room!" I fancy you exclaim. Do you know what a lizard is? Perhaps you have seen a creature about four or five inches long, with four feet that look almost like hands: they are found in the grass sometimes, and are called efts. These efts are very like the Indian lizards, only the lizards are brighter in colour. I have known young women frightened at these creatures; I have seen them screaming, and refusing to go into a kitchen where one had been brought in with the wood, and crying themselves into fits almost. They would think that a very hard place where the efts came into their bedrooms: and no one supposes that, harmless as these creatures really are, it can be pleasant to have a lizard or an eft crossing over one's face or nestling into one's throat when one is asleep. But the priest with our army in India welcomes the lizard in his room, and is well pleased to find him take his part against the musquitoes. Snakes are very disagreeable things; human beings seem to have a natural abhorrence of a snake. But there is no way of keeping the snakes out of the hut provided in India for the priest. It is true that these snakes are not all venomous, but some are. At night they are found in the bed-clothes. You place your hand under your pillow after the light is put out, and the damp cold coils of this disagreeable reptile are felt winding round your arm. There is real danger here, besides extreme discomfort. Of course the priest takes every care that no venomous reptile shall conceal itself about him, and then he trusts to God for preservation. And to free himself from the annoyance the harmless snakes may occasion, he keeps a large duck in his room: for this duck kills the snakes; and through the night the creature strides about, now and then uttering a loud " quack," as the battle with a snake ends in victory. Then the animals carried about with the army make their various noises close by,—the dogs bark, the cocks crow; there is no peace during these Indian nights for our English priest.

He gets up between four and five o'clock in the morning, walks to a river that is near, and has a refreshing swim. He then goes his hospital round, and looks after all the men who are sick, and gives them consolation and instruction. He gets back to his hut about nine, and has a cup of tea and a biscuit for breakfast. Then his own reading and writing and study begins. But as the heat will increase as the day goes on, and as it is necessary to keep out the terribly hot air from the little hut in which he lives, he first shuts up door and window, and only leaves just opening enough uncovered to let in light sufficient to work by. Here, and during this time, he receives frequent visits. He is glad to see those who come. All come on business: some to confession—how welcome they are! the priest receives them, thanking God;—some come for advice—they too are welcome; some come to tell him he is wanted directly at the hospital. Out he goes into the strong silvery light and almost burning heat. It is only at the risk of life that some people go out at this hour. But this priest has a soul at rest, and a body never fevered by any luxuries. He drinks neither wine, nor beer, nor spirits. Tea and coffee, almost cold, and dry biscuit—this temperance helps to keep him fit for his work. When one o'clock comes, the priest has his dinner. Then the very hottest hour of the hot season I am writing of is come. Every thing is still, even the dogs cease to bark; every body tries to keep quite quiet. As the priest sits, the heat increases; he is covered with wet, as if he had just left his bath. The moisture runs from him, though he does not move. Then he does what every body else does; he lies down, and perhaps sleeps. And this is a quieter sleep than any he can get at night. Between three and four o'clock he gets up, feeling strengthened, and takes a bath of water, that stands in his room, and

then returns to his studies, and any indoor occupation.
At six o'clock, though it is very hot still, he can go out
again; and he again makes the hospital rounds. He
gets among the soldiers, often finding out Catholics; for
sometimes there are youths in our armies who never
think of what they are till they are obliged to think of
death, and are afraid to meet it: and so the priest walks
about till eight o'clock, when the sun is just gone down;
and he has boiled rice for tea, and keeps ready for any
work that may arise, till about eleven at night, when
the snakes begin to come out again, and the musquitoes
to fly about, and his friends the lizards and the great
duck are ready to help him while he tries to sleep.

You will have observed that this priest has said no
Mass; that great happiness he will not have, perhaps,
till Sunday. It often happens with the army that no
place can be prepared for the great Sacrifice of the Altar
on week-days; so that this priest is not only obliged to
work hard in a trying climate, but he has to give up
what in England has been the great joy of his life. He
has learnt what many people find to be a difficult lesson
—he has given up a good thing. He will say Mass on
Sunday, and he will work hard in that half-dark hot hut
preparing people for Holy Communion, and in that sad
hospital, where men lie fevered, and perhaps wounded
and dying, to prepare them to meet God and make a
Christian end. He rests for about five hours in the
noisy night I have described to you, and for two hours
more in the middle of the melting day; all the rest is
work: and he does it all of his own free-will, for the
love of our blessed Lord, that the souls He died on the

cross to save may not be lost. We must not let this example of diligence and willing service be lost upon us. When we pray for God's blessing to strengthen us to do our own work in this life, let us often thank God for the hard-working priests of the Church, and ask Him to bless us with many more.

"Oh, dear me!" said Anne Wilton, with a deep sigh, when Mrs. Maitland had done, "this is the hardest of all the virtues, I really believe. Diligence means so many things: I must be orderly and steady, with a strong heart and a good will, and a constant perseverance. How one virtue attends another! and we are obliged to practise several in order to be perfect in one. Shall I ever be diligent?"

"Put your heart into it," said a voice close by. The girls looked back, and there stood Father Francis the priest. "That is the way, Anne Wilton,—that is the way. Put your heart into the work, and you will be diligent. And, my dear children, above all things, be diligent to save your souls."

CHAPTER IV.

KINDNESS.

"I HAVE more time than usual to spare. We will take an interesting subject," said Mrs. Maitland—Kindness.

Whoever loves God will love his neighbour also. This we know by frequent teaching, and by observation and experience. If we love God, we shall prove our affection by our actions. So kindness to those who are around us is the natural fruit of a Christian's love of God.

But many persons lead Christian lives, and pray to God, and make acts of hope and love, and yet very frequently transgress the law of kindness—they often transgress from mere thoughtlessness; from selfishness, too, sometimes: and in order to guard against this failing, which often disedifies our neighbours, and makes our own hearts grow hard, we will now think about kindness, and mention some of the ways in which people are unkind to their neighbours; and this will show us how easy and beautiful a practice kindness is, how becoming to the Christian, and how necessary to ourselves, if we would really adorn our holy religion by our good lives. Kindness means love. It is that amount of love which we ought always to have ready to give to our neighbour, and with which we must encourage ourselves when we are doing our neighbour's work, or governing or directing our neighbour's actions.

Every day, and a great many times a day, we can show this love; from morning till night, and sometimes from night till morning comes again, we can be kind; and when we are kind for the love of God, kind because we so love God that we feel obliged to be kind to those whom He has made, then we do great good to our souls, and fulfil the law of kindness in the best possible way.

But there are many, as we said before, who are not kind because they are thoughtless, and some because they are selfish. It is very easy to understand this. I am sorry to say that instances come before us daily.

"O Mary, Mary," said a sick woman once to a young girl who had just been hired to help to wait on her,—"O Mary, I am shivering with cold; do see if the back-door is open, and do bring me a shawl."

"I'll go directly," said Mary. So she finished the letter she was writing to her mother,—for this happened in the evening after her work was done,—and then she walked up stairs and found a shawl.

The sick woman was holy and meek, and she never said, "Why did you not go directly? I insist on your always attending instantly to my orders,"—she was holy and meek, and said nothing; and then the girl poked the fire, and swept the hearth; and as she stooped, she felt a draught come along the floor, so then she said,

"Oh, I never looked at the back-door;" she went from the room and left that door open. When she got to the kitchen, she found the back-door open, and the kitchen-window open also; so she shut the window first, and then, standing at the door, saw a bird flit by to the top of the great hawthorn-bush, and in a moment such a song! "Oh, the nightingale!" said the young woman; "how lovely, how wonderful!" And then she stood silent and still, and holding the door open, till the bird's strong clear song ceased, and she thought she saw his brown small form pass swiftly through the air away to the oak-tree grove. She then shut the door, and walked up stairs. "What a beautiful fire!" she said, as she walked in. Yes, it might well be a beautiful fire. The cold night-air had been rushing up stairs, and through the door that she had left open; and though the fire was clear, the pale face of the sick woman was blue with cold, and her poor heart was fluttering inside her, and there she lay with the shawl held before her mouth; but the servant-girl never thought of the unkindness she had been guilty of, and the sick woman never rebuked her. The servant sealed her letter, and it soon reached her parents by the post. They said, "How kind of her to write so soon!" and they told the neighbours, and they said, "How kind!" and they told the priest that their daughter had written such a long letter, and was so loving and kind, and he said he was very glad; and even the nuns at the convent, where the young servant had been at school, when they read the letter, and found that she had worked hard to finish all she had to do, and got time to write a long letter to her mother, said that she was kind. But that night a glorious guardian angel stood by the sick woman's bed, and saw that she could not sleep for bitter rheumatic pains, brought on by that cold draught of air; and he knew that she could not lie down for the smartings of her diseased chest, which that night-air had inflamed till it felt like raw flesh; and as he gave sweet thoughts to her soul, and helped her heart to be willing, *he* could not have said that that servant had been kind.

And the girl's guardian angel. Did *he* think her kind? No. He knew that she had had no thought for the suffering soul whom God loved, and whose love for Him He was now trying in the furnace of affliction. Her guardian angel knew that she had added to the pains of a soul who loved too much to complain, and was too willing to suffer to allow of one word of rebuke being uttered. This young girl was not kind.

Kindness in words is often forgotten. Words are like a sharp sword; they cut very deep sometimes. A rude push and a rough cry, "Get away now! what are you doing here?" has hardened many an innocent child's heart. "Well, what a trouble you are grown! why you are as helpless as a baby!" has often brought tears to the eyes of weak old age. "Don't stay in the house all day. You are always in the way. You must not keep in like this, even if you can't find work." Such a speech has driven many a boy, not able to get work for a time, out of his home into the alehouse, with any bad companions he may find about the streets. Never say unkind words such as these. And when you hear others use them, be kind yourself. Find something out of the Christian charity that lives in your own heart to make amends for such unkindness. Tell the child to come to you, and do something to keep its innocent little heart from dwelling on the injustice done it;

by some gentle, reverent, loving act prevent the aged soul from feeling mortification; and find some pleasant thing for the good youth to do, who would work if he could, to prevent his feeling the trouble and disgrace of idleness. A kind heart is always a clever one. It will never be at a loss for a kind action when it has the wish to perform one.

No kind person will ever ridicule any personal defect. Kindness never scoffs at a deformed person, or laughs at a cripple, or makes game of a dwarf.

These things are afflictions. They are not things to be laughed at, or treated with any unkindness; for unkindness under such circumstances is cruelty. We should feel tenderly towards all afflicted persons, and study to prevent their feeling distressed; and very humble we should feel. It is not on account of any good that is in us that we have been given perfect forms and strong limbs. God has been very good to us; let us be kind and respectful to others.

But the most shocking unkindness is when unfeeling and unkind persons laugh at an idiot. An idiot is a solemn thing. This world must be a sad place for one who has no mind to fix on Heaven, and no power to meditate on God. But think for a moment what death may do for an idiot. Do you not fear that people who have always had the full possession of their senses, but have offended God, and put religion to shame, and crucified our Lord afresh, will wish at the Day of Judgment that they had been born idiots? It is better to live an idiot than to die in mortal sin. Never, then, be unkind to the afflicted. Our Blessed Lord, when He was on earth, made the lame walk, and the dumb speak, and healed the leper, whom all men fled from. Those who are unkind to the afflicted are unchristian in their conduct, and forget the example of our God and Saviour Jesus Christ.

There is another sort of unkindness, and its name is *spite*. There is something so mean and paltry in all spiteful actions, that there will be no need to say much about them to the readers of this book. A spiteful girl is a person despised by those who find her out or suffer from her. But one way of showing this sort of unkindness shall be mentioned. If you will read the following little story attentively, you will be able to find out through your own good sense and reflection what sort of unkindness is meant.

Jane Dark was a girl who got her living by embroidery. Anne Day got her living in the same manner. They were good Catholic girls. Jane had been saving for some time to buy herself a good warm wool shawl. She had saved for more than a year, when one day she received a present from a lady, and this present enabled her to buy her shawl at once. On the following Sunday she appeared in a good plaid wool shawl; the colours were well chosen, not too light and not too gay. When Anne saw Jane with this comfortable shawl, she felt any thing but kind, though she loved Jane, and had known her many years. So she said,

"How do you do, Jane? What an ugly shawl! How could you buy such a fright as that?"

Poor Jane! Her cheek grew pale. Had she really saved for above a year and spent the lady's present in a thing that was too ugly for any one to like? Jane could not help feeling unhappy. And Anne saw that she felt so. Every one can name this foolish Anne's bad fault. She was jealous and spiteful, and you know she was not kind. And, really, if all the truth must be told, she was uttering a falsehood: for the shawl was not ugly; it was good, respectable, and decidedly pretty; and Anne knew it. But a really kind person would not have said that the shawl was ugly, even if she had thought so. She would have admired its warmth and its quality, and hoped that Jane would always wear it with satisfaction, instead of trying to destroy the girl's pleasure in the fruit of her honest saving.

There are some occasions when kind persons appear to so much advantage that we are grateful and admiring, and cannot help showing our thankfulness for them. Perhaps many of you, for whom this book is written, will get your living in service,—perhaps in some gentleman's great house, as cook, or housemaid, or nurserymaid, or any thing else. Perhaps if that gentleman lives in London, or near any great town, he will give his family change of air by taking them into the country or to the seaside. When you get to the lodgings, or furnished house, which your master has hired for a few weeks or months for his family, you will not find every thing in the high order you have been accustomed to in the great house at home. And what will the consequence be? Some persons would act in this way. They would grumble, wonder how any one could possibly expect them to do their work in so inconvenient, so ill-furnished a place; and make every one more uncomfortable than necessary, and be, in fact, teachers of discontent. They would find trouble and trial in every thing. Other people would be kind, that is, they would do as all kind people do—they would make the best of every thing. Difficulties disappear from these persons' paths. They are cheerful, full of clever contrivances; and it is wonderful how clever kind people always seem to be; they soon find that things are not so very bad, that they can easily make things do, that thousands of people manage their worldly affairs every day with fewer conveniences than are there; and that it is, on the whole, a good thing to rough it a little sometimes; it teaches people to do with less, and not to be so much in bondage to luxuries. Very thankful has many a good mistress felt to those kind and clever people—clever, because out of the willing depths of their loving hearts they have found a remedy for evil, and proved the truth of a good old saying, "Where there's a will, there's a way."

And in those great troubles of life, in those sad hours of sorrow, which no earthly power can mend, which can be cured by no human tenderness, do you think kind people are not wanted then? More than ever then do we value the true kindness of a Christian heart. Then we find out what we have not perhaps thought of under smaller trials; we find out that the true spring of real kindness is the love of God, as this chapter began by saying, that those who love God love their neighbours also. It is because God so loved us as to redeem our souls by dying on the Cross, and because our souls are kept alive in this love by the adorable Sacrament, that our hearts fill with kindness towards all around us. When we feel this kindness growing cold, when we think of our neighbour's sorrows, and "*don't care*," let us suspect ourselves. Surely no one who feels the love that flows in the Sacrament of Penance, where our sins are forgiven, and is so strong and so wonderful in the Blessed Sacrament, where God gives Himself for the food of our souls, can ever be wilfully unkind to any of those for whom our Lord died, and for whom He lives again; whom He loves with a kindness that no creature can fully comprehend.

You shall now have a story of an extraordinary act of kindness, which will help to fix what has been said in your memory.

Three sisters were once left orphans. The two eldest were called Jane and Kate. Their ages were nineteen and twenty. The youngest, who was called Mary, was only fourteen. As the elder ones could get their living by taking in dress-making and plain-sewing, they went to live in a pretty country village; where their aunt, who was a widow without children, lived in a nice cottage with a flower-garden in front, and an orchard at the back. She was not rich, and yet not poor; for she had good health, and she worked at the squire's two days in every week; and she took in a lady's washing, and kept poultry, and had a pig, and every year sold large quantities of apples; and she grew potatoes, and cabbage, and turnips, and mangel-wurzel, in those places in the orchard which were not shaded too much by the trees. This woman's name was Anne Tarleton,—Dame Tarleton, she was generally called,—and she was a very good woman, and very generally liked. When her nieces were left to take care of themselves, she said that she would take Mary to live with her; and so Mary went to Dame Tarleton's cottage, and made herself useful both out-doors and in-doors; and she wrote copies and did sums in the evening, and made clothes for her aunt, and satisfied her perfectly. Mary did not forget her religion. Every day she read a little in a book, which no doubt many of you know,—a book called "The Imitation of Christ." And Mary really did what many people do not do: she opened her book daily with reverence, collected her thoughts, made the sign of the Cross, and said, "O Lord, help me to understand, and to practise what I read;" and then giving one thought to her guardian angel, and another to the blessed Virgin whose name she bore, she began to read. All this did not take a minute; but Mary did it every day. And often the reading did not occupy two minutes, for she led a busy life. But what she gained in those two minutes, she treasured in her heart faithfully. She read in the morning, and she gave an instant's recollection to what she had read, two or three times in the day. Her example is a good one; and I hope that there are many of us who do as she did. There were a good many Catholics in the village and in the neighbourhood; and the chapel was about half a mile off, and close by the chapel there was a school. Mary had often wished to teach some of the small children. She thought she should like teaching; but she was modest and humble, and never mentioned her wish.

At last Mrs. Darwin, the mistress, said to her, "Mary, you are a well-taught girl. You have made your first Communion. You could help me, I think. Take that smallest class, the children who can't read, and teach them the catechism by word of mouth." This was great happiness. Mary sat down; had the little creatures to sit round her, took the smallest on her knee, and kept another little creature quiet by her side by putting her arm round her. The children got on very well; but Mary observed that a girl, a stranger to her, loitered into the school Sunday after Sunday, and stood staring and watching her; and this was rather a distraction to her, for the girl was quite as big as she was, and looked even older.

After a few Sundays, the gentleman whom they called "the Squire" came into the school, and he saw Mary. "Mrs. Darwin," he said, "I don't think it well to give that child a class to teach; she is too young."

Mary was small and delicate-looking, and looked much younger than she was.

"She teaches well, sir," said Mrs. Darwin.

"Very likely," said the squire; "but teaching at that age so often makes girls vain and conceited. Is there no young woman who would take that class? Have you spoken to Father Francis?"

"No, sir, I did not ask Father Francis. I did it of my own authority. Father Francis only came home on Friday."

And from this conversation a change arose in the arrangement of the classes; and Mary was told to give up her young children to a person older than herself.

Mary was very sorry, even mortified. But she had learnt how to bear humiliation out of her good book, and she gave up the children without a murmur.

Then the tall girl, who had confused Mary sometimes by her loitering listening ways, said,

"Teach me."

"Teach you!" said Mary smiling; "I couldn't do that."

"Why not?"

"Because you are older than I am, and wiser too, no doubt."

"I can't tell my letters."

"Are you a Catholic?"

"Yes."

"Were you never at school?"

"Never."

"You can say your catechism?"

"No, I can't."

"Have you never been taught any thing?"

"Never. I want you to teach me by word of mouth, as you taught those little ones. I can say some of it;" and the girl repeated the first page of the questions and answers in the catechism.

That Sunday, before night, Mary had learnt every particular about her new acquaintance. And this was the girl's history. Her parents had been Catholics. They were both dead; and she had been sent to the poorhouse, to be kept till she could earn her living. Because she knew she was a Catholic, she would not listen to any teaching she got there; and, indeed, there was very little to be had of any kind. But she was an active child and liked work, and made herself so useful that she was employed in the house, and might have stayed on like a heathen, only that one of the visiting magistrates saw her, and said that she ought to be sent out into the world to get her living. About this time a woman, who got her living by making door-mats and selling them, wanted a girl to help her, and she applied to the parish for a child. This woman lived in the village in which Mary lived; and the girl, who was called Sally, came, the first Sunday that she had leave to go out, to the Catholic school; and feeling shy, and finding Mary sitting with her class near the door, she never advanced any farther, but stood near, watching and listening.

Peg Oakeley, with whom Sally lived, was a woman of a most violent temper. She was not a Catholic, and, indeed, was quite ignorant of all religion. She had been a poor-house girl herself; and if she had ever learnt any thing thère, she had forgotten it. While Sally worked hard she was pleased and quiet; but if her gains were not as much in the week as she had expected, or if Sally wished for a single hour's holiday, she would fly into such passions that she was like a mad woman; and she had already beaten Sally most severely many times, and treated her cruelly in other ways.

Yet, on the whole, Sally liked living with Peg Oakeley better than the workhouse, though she was very much afraid of her. And now that Mary had begun to teach her, she was determined to bear any thing rather than leave the place.

Sally was such an ignorant creature that teaching her was very hard work. Learning her letters was easy, and even reading words of three letters was soon accomplished, and the first chapter of the catechism she had got by heart without so very much trouble; but the real difficulty lay deeper. Mary found it very difficult to make this poor ignorant girl understand that she was to forgive injuries, to return good for evil, and never to tell a lie, or be dishonest, or fall into great passions, or swear, or call names, or take God's holy Name in vain. Mrs. Darwin took pains with Sally, and Father Francis instructed her. But it used to make Mary's heart ache to hear that poor girl's language in the village-street when she was angry.

But prayer and patience and never-tiring kindness did so much, that at last Sally could go to confession, and did really try to lead a good life, and was preparing for her first Communion.

And now happened an extraordinary act of kindness on Mary's part.

It was late in August. The harvest-fields were full of people, and the squire allowed the people in the village to glean on his farm. "Leave something for the gleaners," he used to say as he walked among the sheaf-binders; and many of the poor got large quantities of corn owing to the squire's generosity.

It was a delightful change for Sally; she enjoyed gleaning for Peg Oakeley very much. But Mary, who was gleaning for her aunt, had often to remind her that it really was work though it looked so pleasant, and that she must not waste her time with the poppies and purple corn-flowers, but do her duty towards her employer.

The last day of gleaning, Mary's aunt, Dame Tarleton, told her that she should have all that she could glean for herself.

"You know," she said, "the corn is valuable to me: my poultry are expensive to me in the winter; but, as I can't afford to give you money, I'll let you earn a little. Work hard to-day, and we will measure the grain, and I will buy it of you, and then you can subscribe with the money to the new library kept at Mrs. Darwin's. I hear so much of the books. We will find time for some reading this coming winter."

This was just the thing to please Mary. She was delighted with the plan; and very early she was up on that last morning, to be off to the harvest-field with the first gleaners that passed by. She had picked up a large bundle before noon-day; and then, sitting down to rest for an hour, she remembered that she had not seen Sally. When five o'clock came, she still had not seen Sally. She asked about her of some of the women, and they said she had come to the field about two o'clock, but they had not seen her since. Mary was among the very last to leave the field; and as she sat on the stile lifting her heavy burden of corn, she saw Sally running towards her, looking very hot and odd.

"Sally, Sally, what is the matter?"

"Oh, that old wretch—"

"Hush, no names."

"Well, Mistress Peggy Oakeley, if you like that better. Peg, I say, sent me to the town, six miles, this morning, carrying door-mats, and to bring home hemp."

"Well?"

"I went, and got back before two."

"Well?" said Mary again, looking anxiously at Sally's angry face, and wishing to calm her excited manner.

"Then that old woman had no morsel of dinner. She stuffed a piece of dry crust into my hand, and told me to take a drink of the spring in the road on the way to the harvest-field—and I half dead with the walk and the burden."

"And you came to the harvest-field?" said Mary.

"I did, and thought I would rest in the shade for five minutes; and, believe me," said Sally, with a laugh that she could not restrain,—"believe me, I slept till the gleaners passing on their way home woke me."

"And then you went home?"

"Yes, and found Peg in a passion."

"Where was the corn?"

"I had no corn; but I could not tell her that. She had almost broken my arm with the mop-handle."

Here Sally showed an arm all red and blue with the blow.

"And what did you say?" asked Mary sighing.

"That I had plenty of corn; and that I had only run home for a cord to carry it with. And now move quickly from the stile; I am going into the field to unbind a sheaf and help myself."

"You must not," said Mary. "You have told a falsehood, and now you are going to steal. Sally, you must not."

Mary spoke in vain. There was a small bit of

ground belonging to a very poor man close by, and there this poor old creature had some corn bound up; and though there was not much, it was of great value to him. Another stile was at Mary's right hand, which led into this poor man's garden and corn. Before Mary could guess at what Sally would do, she had jumped over this stile, had filled her arms with the man's corn, and, climbing the hedge at the further end of the garden, was running away towards home.

Mary sat still, wondering what she should do. She did not want Sally to be found out; she did not want this poor man—and he was really poor—to lose his corn. She thought of his mortification on discovering the loss; she thought of all the ill-feeling that would arise, and of the scandal too. But she could not bear to think of Sally being found out and disgraced; a public exposure would probably harden this poor girl's heart, she was still so ignorant of religion. Mary looked at her corn that was resting on the stile by her side. It was her own; she might do as she liked with it. Half of it,—for she had been very industrious,—half of it would replace what Sally had stolen; then the poor man would suffer no loss, and no inquiry would ever be made about the corn. So Mary unbound her heavy load, took out half, bound up the remainder again, and holding the corn she was going to take into the poor man's little field, she tried to get over the stile. The stones of which the fence was made were rather difficult to climb, and so Mary fell; but she got up again quickly, ran to the corn-sheaves, bound up her own with what she found there, and got quickly back to her own bundle, which was still resting on the stile. She took it merrily in her arms, placed it on her head, and walked home.

"Well," said Dame Tarleton, "you are less busy for yourself than you have been for me. You must have been pleasuring yourself."

Mary laughed, and said, "Perhaps I have." And she laughed; for she thought it really had been a pleasure to prevent inquiry about the missing corn by replacing it with her own.

But a few days after this, it got about that one of the squire's workmen had said that Mary, whom every body thought such a good girl, had stolen some of the poor man's corn on the last day of the gleaning. He had gone to the man about it. They had been to the place, and examined the sheaves, and found that one had been opened, and rebound very clumsily. And the squire's labourer said he had seen Mary at that sheaf; and though he could not see her cross to the stile, because the trees hid her as she crossed, yet he saw her directly after with a large bundle of corn on her head; and she had told his daughter that all she got that day she was to be paid for; and he was sure she had stolen the poor man's corn to make her own bundle bigger. It would take a long time to tell you what a trouble arose in that village out of this: how Dame Tarleton raged; how Mary's sisters were scandalised; how Peg Oakeley laughed at all religion, because the best girl in the village had been accused of a theft; and how Sally came no more to be taught, not liking to hear any thing on the subject. But Dame Tarleton's anger with those who accused Mary troubled Mary most. Mary did not know what to do to keep her from taking her part so loudly; and in a few more days Mary had another trouble. When she had fallen in getting over the stile, she had hurt her knee. She did not think any thing of it at the time; but now it was so very bad that the hurt could not be concealed. She told her aunt, and then said to her,

"And, please, don't say any thing more against that man who accuses me of stealing the corn. I did not steal it; but I did go into the poor man's ground. I did climb over the stile, and I fell down and hurt my knee; but I did not steal the corn. Only I must bear the blame; and you, dear aunt, must please to have patience with them and me."

Dame Tarleton stood still like a person stupefied; but she was too frightened at the sight of Mary's bad knee to say any thing more at that moment. The doctor came, and said Mary must lie on a bed all day. Her knee was very seriously injured.

"I will lend you a little bed to put here on this side of the kitchen," he said; "it will not take more room than a sofa. But, Mrs. Tarleton, if your niece is not taken care of, she may die of this knee." This he said to Dame Tarleton privately. She was very sorry; for she loved Mary very much.

Soon it got about that Mary was very ill. Many people came to see her; and no more was said for the present about the corn. But Dame Tarleton went to the poor man, and said,

"I don't believe the story. But if you say that you have lost corn, I can afford to make it up; and I'll do so, if you please."

The man answered honestly, "The girl was no doubt in my ground, and meddling with my sheaves, and she could not have been doing any good; that is impossible, of course. But I will tell the truth; I don't miss any corn. I have thrashed it out myself; and though it is but a little, it is as much as I expected."

Mary grew worse and worse; people grew still kinder. She could not stand now; and friends offered to help her aunt, and to sit with her when she was left alone. But one whom Mary wanted most of all never came,—Sally never came near her. So at last Mary told her aunt she grieved about Sally; and Dame Tarleton went to Peg Oakeley, and asked for Sally to sit with Mary. And she put sixpence on the table for Peg, and said,

"The girl shall have her dinner, and she ought to come twice for that."

So Sally was sent to sit with Mary; and she entered the room so timidly, and looked so odd, that Mary called out,

"Here I am, Sally, on the bed in this corner; don't you see me?" Sally came to the bedside slowly, and stood looking at Mary with a very hard forbidding look. "Sally, give me your hand." She gave it. "Stoop down and kiss me, Sally." Sally kissed Mary, and burst out crying. "Don't cry; we are alone, and I have a great deal to tell you. I want to tell you how I got my bad name and my bad knee." Mary smiled. "Under the bed is my bonnet-box; pull it out, and sit down upon it by the pillow, and let me play with your hand, and kiss me again. Oh, I love you, Sally, and you love me."

"I ought not to love you; I am wicked. I wish I had never come to this place; I wish I had never seen you," said Sally sobbing.

But Mary quieted her, and told her quickly the whole truth about the corn and about her knee.

"But what am I to do? Peg would kill me if I were to say it was me. Look here;" and she pushed up the sleeve of her gown, and showed horrible marks of black and blue. "She would have cut my head open, killed me perhaps, last night, if I had not caught the blow on my arm, and for no fault of mine. I never can say that I stole the corn."

"You need not say it," said Mary. "What I did, I did of my own accord, and I must take the consequences of my own act, and I am willing to do so. But I want you to be sorry for having offended God by the sin of stealing; and when you are sorry, you will resolve never to do the like again. And then you will go to confession with a good spirit, and God will forgive you. That is what I want."

"But I am in a miserable state of mind," said Sally, "and I feel as if I knew nothing. How do I know that God is offended? How should He care?"

"He cares because He loves you. If I want you to be good because I love you, how much more must He want you to be good, who loves you better, ten thousand times and more, than we can possibly imagine!"

"Oh, you love me; but you are sorry about your knee of course, and so am I," said Sally, trying to change the subject. But Mary would not change.

"Sally," she said, "I love you so truly that I am not sorry for my knee, while there is any hope of your learning, through my pain, how to make a really good confession, and so getting the forgiveness of God, who suffered more for you than I can ever suffer, and loves you more than any human being can love."

"And you are quite willing to suffer all this pain and reproach for me?" asked Sally.

"Yes, quite willing. Only I want you to become good and make a good confession, and be always watchful over yourself, and regular at your duties."

Sally went away very thoughtful that day. She came again, however, and came as often as Peg allowed her to come. But Mary did not talk to her any more about being good. She only asked her to read a Litany now and then, and made her go on writing copies, and began to teach her figures. Yet Mary prayed for Sally. And the suffering in her knee increased daily, and the doctor said she was very ill. Sally had to touch the bed-clothes very gently when she made Mary's bed look smooth and tidy: and now Mary would often turn her head and lay it on Sally's shoulder, and cry silently.

"Is it your knee?" Sally would ask, crying too.

And Mary would sob out her answer, "Yes; it is about that that I cry. I can't help it, Sally; but don't tell Aunt Tarleton that I cry."

"Do you ever hate me?" sobbed Sally.

"No, never; I love you dearly, better than ever. I pray that you may be good." Then, once or twice, Mary said, "I shall be better next week;" and Sally did not understand this. And one Sunday evening,

Mary said, "Don't come and see me till Tuesday, Sally."

And Sally said, "Is Father Francis coming to you to-morrow?"

And Mary said, "Yes."

And Sally asked, "Why may I not come in the evening?"

But Mary only repeated, "Don't come till Tuesday, please."

So on Tuesday afternoon Sally came; and as she entered Dame Tarleton went out of the house, and she saw her through the diamond-pane window, sitting on the bench just below it, and knitting a gray stocking. Sally went to Mary's bed, and saw she looked very hot and flushed, and there was only a light coverlid on the bed, for the afternoon was hot.

"How are you?"

"Better," Mary answered; but her voice trembled so oddly, and there was a throbbing in her throat.

"How is your knee?" whispered Sally; for her heart had begun to get softer, and she felt ashamed and penitent now when she spoke of the bad knee.

Mary only smiled. Sally just placed her hand lightly on the bed—and oh, what a cry she gave! There was no leg under that light covering. The doctor had cut off the leg above the knee the day before, on that Monday when Sally had been told not to come.

Then, on her knees, she hid her face in her hands, and could not look on Mary. "Do you love me now?" cried Sally very loudly; for her miserable heart had lost all command of itself, and she cried aloud for grief, "Do you love me now?"

"Better than ever, Sally, dear Sally; you are very sorry now."

And Sally was really sorry. She was touched with true sorrow for sin, and she was sorry because sin offended God. And when she thought of the love of God, and all God had done for her, she wondered how she ever could have done wickedly, and she prayed heartily for grace to live a holy life, and never offend God any more. The very next day she made a good confession.

By the light of this good Mary's kindness, Sally discovered the burning Heart of Jesus, and her own hard heart melted in the flames of its love.

Here we might stop, for enough has been said to show how kindness should be valued, and practised as a sweet duty, because the practice of it makes us like our blessed Lord.

But you may be pleased to know more of these girls. Mary recovered so as to go about on a crutch, and Sally was not contented with her confession to God's priest. She told to every one how she had stolen the corn, and how Mary had suffered for her fault. Old Peg Oakeley was so touched by the story, that she repented of her violent passions, and her hard ignorant life became dreadful to her. She went to the priest for instruction, and within the year became a Catholic.

Sally lived happily with her after this; and as Peg gave up drinking, and many extravagant practices, they got on well in the world, and opened a small village-shop, which proved a very successful business. Three years after Mary's leg was cut off, she died of consumption. And if people had been asked after her death, who the best girl in the village was, I think they would all have said that there was no better girl than Sally.

"Oh, how great a thing is kindness!" said these young girls, when Mrs. Maitland had finished her story,—" how great, how good, how heavenly is kindness and long-suffering!"

Perhaps they had never before thought this. But now they will never forget it. They will always try to remember that our love to each other is a reflection of the love of Jesus for us all. They bid Mrs. Maitland good night, and thanked her lovingly, and went home saying silently, "Spirit of benignity, goodness, long-suffering, and gentleness, have mercy upon us."

CHAPTER V.

DRESS.

No one can deny that dress is a very interesting subject to every young woman; and it is a subject of real importance, and one that ought to be properly understood.

To young women who are earning their living in the world dress is a serious matter. To have good clothes is not only desirable, but even necessary, if they are to get and keep good places. So clothes become a part of a poor girl's fortune; a very important part of her property, on which her success and well-doing may in a great degree depend.

"Yes, that is very true," said Mary Hardy. "We all remember Celia Johns: she was out of a place so long, that she had to pawn her clothes; and then she could not get any one to take her, because she looked so like a beggar; I think she married drunken Jem Jones just for a home,—and such a home! Oh, Mrs. Maitland, don't you remember Jane Sparks? she wore her good clothes all out, and used to borrow her cousin Emma's boots to go to Mass on Sunday: ah, poor Jane!"

"What is become of her?" asked Mrs. Maitland. "I did not know that she was in distress."

"She is better off now; she works by the day at

the Blue Boar. She is very good. But please to go on, ma'am; we interrupted you."

Proper clothing may, then, be ranked among the necessaries of life, said Mrs. Maitland. And to work for all the necessaries of life, and obtain them,—good clothes included,—is right and praiseworthy, and what it is hoped you may all succeed in doing. But there is a question to be answered about dress, as about some other things, and the question is this,—What is suitable to me? Every woman possessed of proper feeling and good sense answers that question to herself in some way. What is suitable to me, to my circumstances, and to the work I am going to do? Though these questions are not being asked in words, they are yet being asked and answered in the hearts of all sensible persons around us every day. It is only the ignorant and the foolish who never ask, and can't answer, these questions; and who are induced to make themselves ridiculous by persons as weak-headed and ignorant as themselves, or, what is far worse, who are led away by the wicked. Now consider this question of dress very seriously; for, indeed, to all young women in this country it is a serious question, and it ought to be understood.

It was not such a serious question in former days. Then custom fixed what sort of dress a woman should wear, and she wore it all her life; just as her mother had worn it before her, and just as those who came after her would continue to wear it. There were no fashions; even great ladies wore the same kind of gowns for many years. And certainly from generation to generation all the active, respectable working classes kept to one kind of dress, and were honestly proud of their condition, and very fond of the dress that told to all the world about them that they won their bread by their own strong hands and clear heads and steady characters.

These dresses would perhaps look a little strange to our eyes now, but they were not ugly. It is not natural to a woman to wear what is ugly. A dress was used because it was convenient to work in, generally suited to the seasons of the year, and pleasant to the eye. We know what the dress was in some places. A red petticoat; a dark slate-coloured bodice above it, with sleeves to the elbow; a large handkerchief of check linen in summer, and of some warmer material in winter, which was fastened down to the bottom of the long waist in front and back; a white apron, or, on common occasions, a coloured one, but always an apron tied over the handkerchief; gray stockings; black shoes; and no bonnet, but the hair drawn back, very much as the hair is worn now, and a white handkerchief, folded, and pinned on the head; so that it protected the neck, and in cold weather could be brought over towards the face, and fastened under the chin. When we see this in pictures, we say, "How pretty!" And no doubt it was very pretty and very sensible, and much less trouble than the sleeves, and collars, and muslins, and frills, and bonnet-caps, and bits of ribbon, and little painted flowers, and wires, and whalebones, and bobbins, and strings, and fancy buttons, and brass brooches, and gilded ear-rings, and trolloping cotton-lace, and glittering little beads, and gauze veil, and velvet neck-band, and painted neck-pin, and elastic bracelet, and fine parasol,—not to mention the necessary articles of dress upon which so many odds and ends are fastened,—in which a number of young women think it very fine, and almost necessary, to dress themselves in the present day. You may depend upon this, that dress is a great deal more trouble, more expense, and occupies many more thoughts now than it did then; and that women do not look one bit the better for it.

In Ireland you may still see in some places the remains of this unchanging woman's dress. In Italy the dress of the country people, which has never changed for hundreds of years, is something of the same sort as I have described, and is extremely pretty. And there are places in France where the old dress is still preserved by rich as well as poor; and though very unlike any dress you ever saw, it is very beautiful.

But the old customs that we used to have in England about dress are gone out of use, and we are not going to try to bring them back. And this only makes the subject of dress a more serious one to each of you; because, instead of having the dress you are to wear settled for you by a good old custom, which you would not wish to break, you really have, in a great measure, to settle the question for yourselves. Each one of you, as you go out in life, will have to answer the question of what is suitable for you to wear in that place in the world which the good providence of God has chosen for you. Perhaps you think that this is a very serious way of putting the thing. But every thing that a Christian girl has to do is serious. People say that there is a right and a wrong way of *doing* every thing,—so there is a right and a wrong way of *deciding* every thing. So now let us think a little of dress, that you may decide about it properly.

Let me begin by saying to you, Don't be a coward. But what has courage to do with dress? perhaps you ask. It has a great deal to do with it.

If a girl makes a certain amount of money every year clear, after food and lodging and washing is paid for, she must be brave and make up her mind as to how much of that money she will spend in dress. She must be brave, for she will see one girl with a bead-trimming, and another with a fine bracelet, and a third with a brooch, and a fourth with a pair of coloured boots, and perhaps she will feel in her heart that she would like to have all those things herself very much. Now I say, you must be brave,—you good, sensible, well-taught Catholic girls, who are reading this book, *you* must be brave,— brave with that strong moral courage which is a woman's greatest power and her best strength; for religion is at the root of this moral courage, which she must be brave and use.

She must reckon her money, and she must remember what she has to do with it.

If she spends the whole, and then is sick, and has to beg for charitable help for the time of sickness, she has degraded herself.

Mind, there is no degradation in poverty, or in begging, when the poverty can't be helped; for then it is God-sent, and is an appointed trial; and if borne well, it greatly benefits the soul. But if a girl, having earned her food, lodging, and washing, and having money in hand, spends all that money foolishly, and then falls to begging, she has degraded herself. What must she do, then? She has reckoned her money perhaps, and determined to buy a gown for a best one. Perhaps she has a friend, a good steady girl in a good place, who has lately bought a very neat and pretty Sunday gown, and looks very nice in it,—perhaps she knows that this gown cost sixteen shillings, making included. But perhaps this girl with the money in her hand has not so much wages, or she has only been a short time in service, and so wants more of other things, and she is not going to spend *all* her money. If this is the case, and that girl, instead of spending sixteen shillings on her gown, buys a pretty good print for six or eight shillings, then she has shown true moral courage, and settled that question well.

If that girl in any way belonged to me, I should be fond and proud of her, and thankful for her too. I should feel sure that she who could be strong on this one point, would be strong on many more. I should watch her walking to Mass in her new print dress, and I am certain it would be of a pretty colour, a nice pattern, properly made, and well put on. And I think that a girl who could begin in this way, would go on in such a manner as to earn a sixteen-shilling gown, or any other suitable thing, before long. But this nice girl will have many good things of her own before the expensive gown is put into her box. She will have good under-clothes.

It is degrading to spend all the money that can be spared on dress on the outside. It too often marks a very disagreeable kind of character. Do you who read this book admire characters who are all outsides? I know you don't. Why should any of you belong to such a class? It is one thing to make the best appearance you can of a respectable kind; but it is quite another thing to make a showy appearance, as if you had so much spare money that to trifle it away in show and finery could be no harm; and all the while not to have respectable changes of linen, or a penny for the poor, or five shillings to help your parents with, or a shilling to buy yourself a good book. Those who give way to the temptation to make a false appearance, will not stop there. They will become false in other things. They will become vain and frivolous and light-minded. Alas for their poor souls, growing starved and destitute all this time! These poor girls are cowards. They have no moral courage, no true bravery, no feeling of the honour that lies in truth,—truth in looks, truth in appearance, truth before their guardian angel and Almighty God Himself.

But now, to go on with this good girl we have been fancying to ourselves. She will have many things in her box before she puts the sixteen-shilling gown there. She will, as I have said before, have good under-clothes, and enough of them.

Many girls cannot keep places, and go home to their poor parents' cottages quite ill and unable to work, for no other reason than because they have no proper changes of their under-garments. They work all day and sleep all night in the same linen. They have not enough to have one change in the week. They have got headaches, are sick at the stomach, and weak in the back; their hands are hot, and their feet cold. They have no appetite, and they are so drowsy in the mornings that it is quite a trial to get up. Now I can assure you, that it is true that these symptoms have all been cured by having good under-garments, and enough of them. It therefore becomes a duty to provide yourself with proper changes. Doing so may keep the pretty gown longer out of your box, as I have said, but you will have your well-chosen, nicely-made, good print dress there; and I would rather see stockings and day garments, and night garments, and warm petticoats for winter, and some light ones for summer, and a nice set of pocket-handkerchiefs, and some neat night-caps, looking white and nice, folded neatly as good things ought to be, and smelling sweet as clean things should;—oh I would rather see that in my nice girl's box than the sixteen-shilling gown; and yet, as I said before, such a girl will have that there too one day.

Now as to finery, we have something to consider about finery. I suppose we may call finery any little thing that is over and above what custom requires to make a respectable appearance. Some people seem to have a natural turn for finery. They have a quick eye for a pretty colour, and they will mix the right colours together, and are what people call "tasty," quite by nature, knowing what will go well together without ever having been taught. And this is really the case. Some people have a natural taste in these things. But like all other tastes, it ought to be kept within proper bounds. There is no harm in it in itself,—no more harm than there is in any other taste or natural gift,—no more harm than there is in knowing one tune from another, and being fond of singing; but, like all other tastes, it must be kept within proper bounds. If you allow the love of colour and the taste for ornament to get the better of you, it will lead you into excesses, and you may have to repent of the consequences as long as you live.

And there is another consideration; and you, as a good Catholic young woman, will understand it perfectly. If you show too much taste for colour and ornament on your own person, you will draw remarks upon yourself. Now Catholic girls will like to possess the friendship of the good, the good opinion of the respectable, and the admiration and love of such persons as *may* admire and love them without risk of offending God; but Catholic girls will not want to be made the objects of common remark. Personal remarks on their clothes and appearance are vulgar and offensive, and proper-minded people are naturally careful not to dress themselves so as to excite these disagreeable remarks. That feeling of self-respect that belongs to all good girls is pained by any thing of this kind, and you will do well to be very particular in avoiding any thing that may lead to painful remarks. Yet there is something exciting in these remarks, and some girls may recollect that they have been made on them, and that they have a little liked them. Now when any girl indulges in such a feeling as that, and is told by her conscience that she has liked being the object of remark on account of her smart dress, and that she has chosen her clothes with a view to keep up this sort of admiration, what do you think she should do?

What—if she were a friend of yours, and told you of these feelings—what would you advise her to do? I know very well what you would advise her to do. I know very well, and I shall write it down to show you that I know. You would warn her that she was giving way to a temptation; you would remind her of the sin of vanity, of the dangers that grow out of this sin; and you would feel afraid for her, and make her feel afraid for herself. Then, as she takes you into her confidence, and lets you advise her, you will advise her to make strong resolutions against this vanity that has so many sorrows in its train; and go with her convictions and her good resolutions to confession; for there she will get rid of the past sin, and get strength against future temptation. Confessing a sin, when it is a little one, is, as you know, like taking a disease in time; it will not be so hard to cure. And when this girl, who has confessed the danger that her love of pretty things has brought her into, goes to her duties, she will get strong enough to fling aside the worldliness she was beginning to love. When she receives her God in the Blessed Sacrament, she will recollect that He is her Master. He is the true object of delight to every Catholic's heart; and for His sake, and for the sake of the Church He planted, and always preserves, and of which He has made her a member, she will give up those things which are pomps and vanities to her. Perhaps, after this, she may even dress a little plainer than she need dress, because she has felt her danger, and found out her temptation. But you need not be afraid that she will look ugly; for you do not think the snowdrop an ugly flower, though it is plain white, or the lovely forget-me-not a fright because it is only blue.

As dress is often a temptation to women, there are some who observe a pious custom about it, which I strongly recommend to you. They pray to the Holy Mother of God, who is the mother of us all, to help them never to give way to vanity, especially in clothes, that they may never give their heart's love to outward finery, but only wear what their station requires, with a holy indifference to the temptations of finery.

I began by speaking of old customs in dress. In the days of our Blessed Lady's life, women wore one fashion of dress. When you see her pictures, you see what it was—a red petticoat, and a blue sort of cloak that formed a veil over the head, and fell down like a mantle round the arms. The dress of our nuns is taken from this. The first nuns wore the dress of the women who saw our blessed Lord, only they chose the soberest colours, as they had for His sake given up the world. Don't let holy nuns, who have perhaps had the teaching of some of you, ever sorrow because you have been led into bad company, and tempted into follies and dangers for the love of dress.

I will tell you now a true story of an English girl, who was young and very beautiful, and whose parents were noble and very rich. It was one of the duties of this young Catholic girl's place in the world that she should go a great deal into company and wear such clothes as belonged to her station. You would have thought she looked like an angel had you seen her ready to go out to some grand party in an evening, so beautifully was she dressed, and so lovely had it pleased the Lord to make her. Of course she was very much admired, and she was so amiable and good that all loved her. Indeed, she was very good, and loved God better than any thing this world had given her, though it had given her so much. Her fine clothes were nothing to her; her bright jewels had no place in her heart; and she wore her diamonds and pearls and lace with as much simplicity as if they had been the white handkerchief and coloured petticoat that I told you of at the beginning of this chapter. She just wore them because it was the custom of the country that people of her rank and fortune should do so. But at last people got to admire her openly, more and more openly; and she got to know it. At first she did not care; then she liked it a little; and at last, one evening, when a wreath of diamonds was put round her head, and she saw how well she looked, she felt emotions of vanity. She was very happy that evening; but when she knelt down to examine her conscience that night, she shed tears, for she had been vain and proud, and desirous of admiration. Though every body had admired and loved her, and spoken of her goodness and beauty, she knew in her heart that our blessed Lord had not been first in her love that night,—that she had loved *herself* and been vain. What should she do? She was going out again the next evening, and again going through the same dangerous temptation. She could not stay at home; it was her duty to go. She could not give up her beautiful ornaments; for it belonged to her station to wear them. What could she do?

The next evening, when her maid was dressing her, she said she would put the wreath into her hair for herself; and so she sent the maid away. Then she twisted small pins into her wreath with the points towards her head; they were not put so as to prick her badly, for then it would all have been found out; but they were so placed as to remind her of her danger, by little pricks round her head that night. Then, in the midst of that bright room, and with so many flattering friends around her, she spent the next hours smiling and dancing and doing all that was required of her. But every minute she felt the wreath prick her, and then she lifted up her heart to God, and said some little prayer, such as this: "O Jesus, who didst wear a crown of thorns for me, give me grace to be humble all my life." Her mother, who knew what a holy child she had, used to talk to her on pious subjects; and one day before her death,—for she died first,—she confessed to her mother what her temptation had been, and how she had overcome it. After her death, her pious relative told the story, and edified many by doing so. It should teach us the danger of dress, and should make us fear lest too great a love of it should unfit our hearts for the thankful contemplation of the sufferings of our blessed Lord.

CHAPTER VI.

GOSSIP.

The next subject was Gossip. Gossiping women! said Mrs. Maitland; every body has heard of gossiping women. And every body has heard these gossiping women called odious, and dreadful, and horrid, and too-bad, and falsehood-tellers, and altogether people that other people would do very well to have nothing to do with.

But how are we to know gossiping women or gossiping men,—for we do not believe that all gossiping is confined to women and girls. We think that men and boys and even little children gossip, and if so ought to be, all of them, avoided. What! avoid children? some one says perhaps. Good children had better avoid gossiping children, certainly; and grown-up people should take the greatest pains to correct them. Every one must think sorrowfully of a gossiping child. It is a sorrowful thing to think of the bad company that child has been in, of the bad examples it has suffered from; for, poor innocent, it was not always a gossip and a scandal-monger.

But how are we to know gossiping people? Some people are pleasant talkers, have a great deal to say, and say it very agreeably. What difference is there between pleasant talking and gossip? And how shall we know an agreeable companion from a gossip?

These are plain sensible questions. And, although it seems to be a very solemn way of beginning, yet the best beginning to an answer to these questions will be by asking another, namely, "What is mortal sin?" This is truly a solemn question; for there is nothing so awful as mortal sin, and nothing so dreadful in its consequences, if committed and never repented of.

"What is mortal sin?" Every one of the readers of these pages can tell perfectly well. Every Catholic can answer that question to their own conscience, and every Catholic who has received instruction can put the answer into words.

Mortal sin, say our holy books,—deadly sin,—is an action by which a person breaks the solemn law of God, and therefore incurs the death of his soul; for "*the soul that sinneth, it shall die.*"

This is an awful thought. We all of us have it in our power to commit actions that must send our souls to everlasting punishment, unless by God's grace we repent of them. But again, perhaps some one asks a question, and a very proper question, What has gossip to do with mortal sin? Such sin is a grave and terrible wickedness, and gossip is only a foolish love of talking; what can mortal sin and gossip have to do with each other? Your question is a very just one, my dear young reader. But if we once more turn to our holy books, we shall soon find more about it.

If we ask how deadly sins are committed, our holy teachers tell us in various ways, but *in this order*—mind, in this order. First, the representation of some sin to the fancy and the intellect, and then great pleasure in the thought of it, and then willingness to commit the sin, and at last the deed itself. And if this deed is not repented of, and the temptation not avoided, then we generally see that the commission of sin grows frequent, and often becomes a habit, and the soul is fixed in a state of mortal sin. Such, as holy teachers tell us, is the order in which sin is perpetrated and gains its deadly power over the soul. And it is with the first steps of this downward path to sin that gossip has to do.

Gossiping people often, very often, talk of sin,—of its pleasures, and of the worldly advantages that sometimes belong to sin. And they describe sin, and how it has been done, and how other people might do it, till the representation of sin to the fancy is completed, and the intellect comprehends it. This is a great misfortune. And such a gossiper is the worst of mischief-makers. Young and innocent souls are hurt by such gossip; and by and by these young souls find others, and they tell to them what they have heard talked about, and they excite their fancies, and so mischief spreads, and the gossipers do the devil's work.

Now it is certainly true that all of us like to know about things. If any thing happens, we like to know all the particulars; and we inquire into things, and collect evidence, and examine into matters, and take a great deal of trouble to know all about it. We all know that this is natural. We also know that it is often the duty of persons placed in authority to make inquiries about crimes or accidents, or any thing concerning which we expect to be protected by the laws of our country. It is natural to us to wish to know all particulars; but that is no reason for our gossiping over matters which had better not be talked of, and so inflaming our own minds and the minds of our hearers with an interest in wrong things, and a curiosity about sin which ought never to be felt at all. There certainly is something very interesting about little particulars.

If we were to be told a story of a lady in this way, "The day before yesterday a lady was thrown from her horse and killed," we should feel shocked for the moment, but there are very few of us who would really care,—some would never think of the poor lady again. But suppose some one else came in and said, "Oh yes; and she was such a beautiful lady, and she was young, not more than eighteen; and she rode a lovely gray horse,—a horse that looked so gentle, and that she was so fond of, and had had for several years; her brother gave it to her. She has no sisters, and only this one brother, and he gave her this horse; and the horse would eat sugar out of her hand, and take biscuit from her workbasket and fruit from her fingers; and he always neighed when she came into his stable, and he knew her as well as if he had been a dog; and this morning he threw her off, and she is dead." Now should we not all feel very much more interested about this poor lady's accident, and more sorry for her death, because we knew these particulars? Of course we should. And suppose that some one else could tell us still more. "This beautiful horse had not intended to hurt his mistress. A dog had jumped from a hedge suddenly into the road and frightened the poor creature. He did not run away, but stood close by the dead body of the poor young rider, and smelt her hand once, and then trembled terribly, and burst out into a white foam from fear. Poor horse, they led him away shaking, and scarce able to walk. Poor horse, did he know it was death when he touched her wrist with his warm nostril?" Is not our natural interest heightened by hearing this much more? and do we not long to know still more,—and do not some of us say, "Oh, what happened then? where did they take the lady? Oh, tell us more. Had she no one with her? How odd that she should have been quite alone!" Of course we should ask such questions as these. It would be perfectly natural, and quite right to ask them. For, you see, our interest has been greatly increased by the mention of some of the particulars of this lady's death, and we should like to hear some more. Perhaps, then, we are told more. "This lady, to whom we should scarcely have given a second thought but for the particulars which we are always pleased to hear,—this lady must have died immediately. She was flung violently from her horse, and her head fell on a large stone, which forced in a part of the skull. She must have been stunned and killed instantly by the blow; such a short moment from her seat on the saddle to her death-bed on the stone! Who would not store up prayers to our Blessed Lady and the saints to remember us in the hour of our death, when death may come to us as suddenly as it did to this poor girl,—too suddenly to let us pray for ourselves? Well, she was alone; for the servant who had been with her to the neighbouring town had got drunk there, and she had been so frightened at the thought of a drunken man riding after her, that she had galloped away from him, and was trying to get home by herself. This was the cause of her hurry. How will that drunken servant feel when he looks at her dead body, if he ever dares to look at it? Poor young lady! she lies at the little road-side inn, in the room on the left-hand side, and she is in her coffin there. She is to be taken back to-night to her mother's house. Her father died when she was very young, and her mother is lonely now, for the brother is in the army in India. She will be buried next week in the Catholic burial-ground, and young women dressed in white, from the village where her father built the chapel, will carry her to her grave; and many priests will say Mass for her dear soul; for she visited the sick, and helped the poor, and taught the young, and never forgot the dead while she lived; and now hundreds of hearts will pray for her."

My dear readers, this example is sufficient to show how particulars interest us. And there is no harm in hearing particulars such as these; indeed, on the contrary, there may be great edification as well as pleasure in hearing particulars of events that happen around us. But this example will also show how undesirable it is to hear particulars about any kind of sin; telling such particulars is the worst kind of gossiping. It is allowing the fancy to dwell upon what offends God; it is interesting the mind in things which it ought to avoid even thinking about; it is allowing ourselves to have pleasure in hearing about events that ought never to have happened.

It is true, nevertheless, that wrong things are done, and must be spoken of; but such things should be spoken of in a proper manner, and by the person whose business it is to speak of them. When others say one to another, such a thing has been done, such a person has acted wrongly, they should say it without curiosity, without longing to know particulars, without dwelling upon the sin till the heart delights to hear about it; without going from one person to another telling the story again and again, till they enjoy telling it, and would even go out of their way to find some new person to tell it to who had never heard it before. To do this is gossiping, and very dangerous gossiping; for it is spreading the knowledge of sin, and making people's minds familiar with it. There are many persons who might hear of an evil deed, and feel sorrow for the commission of a sin against God, and offer up a prayer for the person in the wrong; and then, it being no particular business of theirs, they might think no more about it, except to make a resolution to avoid bad company, and to help the wrong-doers to repentance, if God ever gave them the opportunity. They would then think no more of it than you would have thought of the story of the lady who fell from her horse, if you had been told no more than the first fact; but if some gossiping person *will* talk to them, *will* tell them names and places and circumstances and occasions,—repeating what one thought and the other said, and who saw them last, and how it all happened in the end,—then that person, whose knowledge of the sin might have ended with an act of sorrow, a prayer, and a good resolution, gets into quite a different state of mind. She hears, and wonders, and grows interested, and asks questions, and is told things she had better not have heard; and instead of good acts and pious prayers, she will find some one to tell it to in her turn; and so for days these people's souls are entertained with thoughts of sin and meditations on other people's iniquities. These people are gossips, and they are doing a great deal of harm; they harden people's hearts, and draw people away from the Christian examination of their own consciences, and make them curious about their neighbour's sins, and pleased and entertained with accounts of them. Just as you were pleased to hear about the poor lady's horse, of where she got it, why she was alone, if she suffered in her death, where her corpse lay, and when and how she would be buried,—just in the same way the human heart, unless kept in restraint, likes to hear the particulars of evil deeds, and is pleased to prolong conversations on such subjects; but this inclination of the human heart *must* be restrained whenever it desires to get better acquainted with any thing evil. Remember this as long as you live. You cannot live in the world without meeting gossiping people: never encourage them. Remember that such conversations as have been now described prepare the mind for evil, and familiarise the soul with thoughts of mortal sin. We can't live in the world without knowing a great deal of sin; for when sin is doing all around us, we can't keep ourselves quite ignorant of it. But we can keep ourselves from thinking of it, and talking of it, and gossiping about it; and it is our duty to keep ourselves from this habit, and to keep others from it if we can; for it is the way of danger, and leads often to sin of the gravest kind.

There are some other sorts of gossiping not so positively wrong as talking about sin; they are, however, if not positively wrong, very dangerous and injurious kinds of conversation. For instance, talking of other people's affairs, of which you can only know a very little, perhaps nothing, and yet of which you talk with as much ease as if you knew every thing; and if you did know every thing, that would give you no right to tell every thing. This is not loving our neighbour as ourselves, or doing as we would be done by.

James Morris, a footman in a gentleman's family, boasted of the beauty of his master's plate; and the house was robbed. He was an untrustworthy person; a man, therefore, not fit for a gentleman to employ,—a gossip. Emma Martin talked to all her friends of her mistress's clothes. She had never before lived with a lady whose position in life obliged her to go out very often. Emma said to her friends that her mistress had sixteen gowns; the friend said that the lady had sixteen *best* gowns; the girl to whom she told it said the lady had *more* than sixteen best gowns—oh, many more,— perhaps ten more; this was in answer to questions when people got interested. The next person said the lady had twenty-six gowns; the next person, that she had scores of dresses—she really believed Emma Martin had said sixty. This story, after having been gossiped about for some time, got back to Emma's mistress. She sent for Emma, accused her of having gossiped about her clothes, and told ridiculous falsehoods; and then she discharged her. And now observe this,—that lady never again kept a maid to wait upon her. She said that she had given up keeping a maid, for they were all such gossips; she preferred waiting on herself, and putting out her needlework. Thus a comfortable place, in which many a good girl had got an honourable living, was closed against all others.

Henry Davis, a young man in a shop, gossiped about the quantities of groceries purchased by the neighbouring families, and told who paid by the month and who paid by the quarter, and how others left their bills to the end of the year, and talked of who burnt mould-candles and who burnt dips, till some families discovered it, and left the shop; and others did as they did, and Henry Davis's uncle, who kept the shop, was ruined, and his gossiping nephew with him.

These are instances of gossiping talk that has no actual sin in it; but yet it is wrong. It is impertinent; such talk is a liberty taken with your neighbour's affairs. We don't wish people to gossip about us; we don't want people to tell to other people, of whom we don't know any thing, what property we have, what clothes we wear, what food we eat, and how we manage our private affairs; why, then, should we tell those things of others that it would be impertinent in other people to tell of us? We must deal honourably one with another. People never act honourably when they are gossiping. Many and serious are the injuries to our neighbour done by this kind of gossiping. Another sort of gossiping is when girls or women, for the sake of mischief, tell of another just the very thing they know in their hearts that that person would rather not have told. Think a moment. Did you ever hear a quarrel between girls and women begin with, "What business had you to say that? What did you tell that for? What right had you to talk about me?" Yes, you have heard many quarrels begin in this way; and many angry passions and fierce feelings and coarse words, and often cruel unforgivingness and wicked oaths and bitter revenge, have followed on this kind of wicked gossip. Never, never be the cause of such sorrow as this. You will answer for it in some way that perhaps you do not often think of, if you do. Do as you would be done by. Remember the mischief that your tongue may do. Consider this: a thief can return what he has stolen; one who strikes another may cure the injured part; but whoever tells of another what ought not to have been told can never repair it. Consider this: you can never bring back the words that have gone forth. If you have injured your neighbour by telling any thing that ought not to have been told, not any thing you can do can repair it. This should make us very careful when speaking of our neighbour; but only a few remember that they may do with their tongues an injury that not even the sacrifice of their lives can make amends for.

In the beginning of this chapter, gossiping children were spoken of. Perhaps some of the readers of this book may have the care of children. They may be nurses, or they may be in schools where young children are, or they may have young brothers and sisters, who may be depending on them for example and teaching.

All people who have observed children know how fond they are of any thing new; how attentive they are to stories that they hear told, and how well they remember them. And yet people treat children as if they had neither eyes nor ears, neither memory nor understanding. In many houses all manner of wicked stories are gossiped over before little children. If grown-up people are ready to listen, of course children, to whom the world is fresh and every thing a novelty, will listen too; and, depend on it, they remember. Tell a child a pretty story, and see how eagerly it will listen; and watch children who, unhappily, are early made acquainted with evil. How soon a little boy in the street will laugh at the gestures of a drunken man; how soon he will be amused at a man in a passion, if the man is not angry with himself; how early he will catch the sounds of oaths, and how quickly he will use them in his play. Do you think that creatures so naturally clever and intelligent will not soon love the mystery of stories told of wrong-doers, and will not by that means early learn what wrong-doing is? It is dreadful to think of the injury that the tongues of girls and grown-up people do to children. How often have we heard little children say, "I know a story of Jemmy, but I mus'n't tell;" or "I know what Mary did, but I sha'n't tell." Why should children know any stories that they may not tell? They soon learn to love gossip, and to be artful and deceitful about it. They soon learn to listen at doors, and to pretend to be asleep in bed when they are awake, and listening with delight to gossiping tongues. Thus they are made deceivers; and if suspected, they will tell a lie to hide what their poor young hearts know to have been wrong.

Keep all temptations of this kind, if possible, away from a child. Keep down all inclination for gossip in your own hearts, and never do or say any thing that may encourage or give birth to the spirit of gossip in a child. There are plenty of things to talk about without dangerously talking of sin, impertinently exposing your neighbour's affairs, or cruelly injuring your neighbour's feelings.

If you should still think that gossiping is a small thing to have had so much said about it, remember what God has said in His written word: "He that contemneth small things shall fall by little and little." And sometimes say this short prayer, "Make me, O Lord, to fly small evils, since great ones are born of them."

CHAPTER VII.

CURIOSITY.

AGAIN the girls met, and a subject was chosen; and Mrs. Maitland began to talk to them of Curiosity.

To be curious, that is, to desire information about matters which are not your concern, and of which, perhaps, somebody may even desire to keep you ignorant, is very wrong. Curiosity is a tiresome, disagreeable fault. Curious people are seldom respected. Every body feels that the curious girl is a mean character; and the most dishonourable and prying acts are often, and not unjustly, attributed to her.

To be curious is not to do as you would be done by. If a fellow-servant receives a letter, why should you be curious to know who it is from, and all that is written in it? If she had wished you to know, she would have told you. If she did not tell you, you should make it a point of honour not to be curious. Curious minds do not always rest contented with wishing and wondering only. The mind does not rest satisfied with wondering; it wants to know, and it will try to learn. This desire for knowledge is a good thing when well directed, and it is a bad thing when directed wrongly. When well directed, it is a praiseworthy desire after improving information; when ill directed, it is a foolish and dangerous curiosity. Thus, you see, there is a wide difference in your desiring to be informed on any useful subject, as, for example, history, and your being curious about the contents of your fellow-servant's letter. Every one can feel the great difference between the probable results of these two feelings. You can encourage one; you can get books, ask questions, and remember and repeat all you learn, both wisely and innocently; but can you read that letter and learn its contents and talk of them? You are ready to say, "No, it would be unkind and dishonourable; it would be doing an injury to our neighbour; it would be a deceit, and like acting a lie. Whoever would do such a thing, ought not to be trusted or respected." I can fancy that you have said this, and felt what you have said in your heart. And thus the girl who gives way to curiosity is certain to be thought and spoken of. Sad mischief often arises out of curiosity. Many faults follow in its train, rash judgments especially.

"Have you seen our new servant?" said a housemaid to a cook one day.

"No; where is she?" said the cook.

"Up-stairs, unpacking her box. She has got such a beautiful shawl. Where could she have got such a shawl? I wish I knew. I can't think where she could have got such a beautiful shawl; I wish I knew."

"Nonsense! don't be so curious; bought it, I suppose," said the cook.

"Bought it!" exclaimed the curious housemaid; "I don't believe that. It looks as good as our mistress's. I always admired that. I always wished to know what she gave for that; and I *do* know now. I saw the shop-bill on the writing-table, and I looked through all the articles, and there was the shawl; it cost —"

"Hold your tongue!" said the cook angrily; "I won't hear what it cost, and you had no business to look. It was a mean, dishonourable trick. Why should you want to know what our mistress gives for any article of dress?"

The cook was angry; the housemaid vexed. But she went to the new parlour-maid's room to talk about the shawl.

"That was some rich person's present, I am sure?"

"Not exactly," said the young woman, as she placed some of her clothes very neatly in the open drawer.

"Not exactly! Well, that is an odd answer."

"What time is the parlour-dinner?" asked the new servant, taking no notice of the other's speech.

"Oh, not till six o'clock. Shall I help you?"

"No, thank you."

"Why, you have got a dressing-gown! I thought servants could do without dressing-gowns."

"It was a present from my mistress once, when I attended her in an illness."

"And then she gave you a present in money, and you bought that shawl? I know now what you meant by saying 'not exactly' when I asked if it had been given to you."

The new servant looked up quite astonished, and feeling very puzzled.

"No," she said, "I had no money. I have had that shawl some time."

Days passed on, and still this curious girl wanted to know something more about the shawl.

When Sunday came, the young woman did not wear the shawl. The housemaid saw her go to Mass. After a little while she went to the bedroom where both of them slept; and as the key had been left in the drawer where she had seen the shawl placed, she was so tempted that, giving way to her curiosity, she opened the drawer to look. There lay the shawl; it really was a beauty. There, too, lay a white lace veil, of very fine lace; there lay a fan, very large, with gilded sides and edges, and bright bits of mother-of-pearl inlaid upon it. She then, still overcome by her curiosity, moved some things, and saw three real cambric pocket-handkerchiefs, and a name which did not belong to the new servant embroidered on them. In putting these things back to their places, her sleeve brushed off the top of a small paper box, and she saw a letter. Now, as curiosity is never satisfied, she opened this letter; and glancing at one of the pages, she read these words: "Respecting the clothes, I feel sorry you have taken them to your place. I am afraid of trouble. You objected to selling them, and yet it might have been the wisest thing to do. The money is safe. I did as you desired about it." At this moment the street-door was opened. The woman replaced the things as fast as she could; and when the new parlour-maid entered the room, she pretended to be brushing her hair. But as she looked at the young woman taking off her straw-bonnet and unfastening a cloth shawl, she thought —alas, what did she think?—she thought, "You are a thief."

This was rash judgment. Why did she not see her own fault? Why did she not in her heart accuse herself of her dishonourable doings, her evil curiosity?—why did she judge a stranger rashly? You see how many wrongs her curiosity had led her into. You see what a bad thing curiosity is.

But it did not end here. A fortnight passed. All this time evil thoughts of her fellow-servant continued in this girl's mind; and as she was still as curious as ever to know more of what she had seen, she began to talk in an artful kind of way, in order to draw some confirmation of her suspicions from the poor unsuspecting parlour-maid.

At the end of the fortnight, she told the cook that she believed the parlour-maid to be a thief:

"I have asked her again and again about that shawl," she said, "and I can't get any thing out of her except that she did not buy it, and that it was *not exactly* a gift. I am sure she stole it," she said angrily, "and other things besides. I do really believe she is a thief."

At first the cook, who was a sensible elderly woman, did not listen to her; but at last the girl confessed that she had looked in the new servant's drawer, and there saw many things that could only have belonged to a real lady; and then the cook got a little uncomfortable, and said she had a great mind to tell her mistress. But the housemaid would not let her do that, because she did not wish her mistress to know that she had looked so dishonourably through the new servant's things.

It happened, in about a month, that the mistress of

the house lost a silver card-case. It could not be found any where. She had used it only a few days before, and she was very much distressed at her loss. When she was ordering dinner one morning, she spoke so earnestly about this loss, that the cook said,

"Well, ma'am, I think it my duty to say, that we have suspected the new servant of being a thief."

The lady started.

"I had an excellent character with her," she said.

"Yes, ma'am; but the housemaid can tell you that she has many things in her possession not likely to belong to a servant. She has lady's things in her box, I hear—things she never wears. I did not think much of it at first; but she never speaks of these things. The housemaid has said from the first that she was a thief, and now that you have lost your card-case, I feel suspicious myself."

The lady thought silently for a little time; then she said,

"I shall part with her. I shall not accuse her. I have not proof enough for that. But what you say makes me uncomfortable. I shall part with her."

So that night the young woman had her month's wages instead of her month's warning, and the next day she was gone. The housemaid quite rejoiced in her heart. Indeed, she had fully persuaded herself of the woman's dishonesty, and all this time had never found out her own fault; or if she had accused herself a little of being dishonourable in opening the drawer and reading the letter, she yet never suspected that she had come to any wrong conclusion as to the woman's character.

The woman, as I have said, went away the next day. It was no hardship, for she had a good home to go to. Soon she offered for another place, and a lady wrote to her former mistress for her character. This lady asked if she was clean, civil, honest, and if she knew her work. The good lady with whom she had lived was puzzled how to answer this letter. But she wrote as well of her as she could, saying she knew her work perfectly, was very clean and civil and obliging, and that she hoped she was honest. But this *hoping* she was honest did not satisfy the lady; and she wrote again to ask why she had been parted with. Then this answer was returned: that she had been discharged on account of some suspicions, which were never mentioned to her, and which made her fellow-servants and her mistress uncomfortable. But her former mistress, though she told the truth thus plainly, added her hope that she would get the place; and said that she had never had any opportunity given her of clearing herself, as she had never been openly accused.

You must observe in what a difficult position the curious housemaid had placed her mistress. This lady did not like to accuse the parlour-maid on evidence so improperly obtained, and yet, through the other woman's curiosity, she had heard enough to discharge her. And so the other lady was placed in a difficulty also. She had young servants in her house. Her parlour-maid had many things of value intrusted to her. She thought for a day of what she should do,—whether she should take her, or whether she should not take her; and she decided at last to have nothing to do with her. And so she lost this place, and then another, and then another; and then her mother had an illness that kept her at home, and was so expensive that it took almost all their money. And then the poor mother died; and the last sovereigns were spent in buying some very plain mourning-clothes and in the funeral.

Then this poor girl fell into great poverty, and really did not know what to do. But she remembered one thing that she could do, and she went to the town where her old mistress lived to do it. In one of the streets, just as she entered the town, she met the cook of whom I have spoken. The cook knew her, and spoke to her.

"You don't look as well off as you used to look," said the cook, in a kind tone of voice.

"I am very much reduced. I have had great trials. I have never been able to get a place since I left your mistress nearly two years ago. Have you got the same housemaid?"

"No," said the cook; "she went a year ago. She was so curious. She did a deal of mischief before she went. My mistress was very angry with her."

Then the cook said, "If you would come back with me, I would speak to my mistress; perhaps she might hear of something to suit you."

So the young woman went back with the cook, carrying a parcel which she had brought into the town. The lady was not at home; so the cook made tea, and they sat down to wait for her return. While they were at tea, the young woman said,

"I am so reduced, that I was going to try to sell

some things that I have had for some time. Will you look at them?"

Then she opened the parcel, and the cook saw for the first time the shawl, the veil, the fan, and the handkerchiefs that the curious housemaid had talked about.

"They were a legacy to me," said the young woman; "a legacy from my aunt. She lived as nurse to an invalid lady;—you may have heard of her; she was Lady Caroline Knightley. When she died, the family gave my aunt her clothes. She sold all but these things. The handkerchiefs and the fan she had used in the lady's last illness, and so had a respect for them. I have heard her say, these three she washed herself after her dear lady was departed; the veil she kept, for she always thought she would drape a little altar to our Blessed Lady with it; and the shawl, which you see is very handsome, she fancied she might wear herself one day. But she died; and at her death she left these things and ten pounds to me, for I was her god-daughter. My mother, at my request, put the ten pounds into the savings-bank. It is all spent now."

"Had you got these things with you when you were here?" asked the cook.

"Yes; I had them here. But my mother was sorry I brought them, and said so in a letter. She fancied that some one might see them, and wonder about them. She had always a fear of falling in with curious people; she used to say they were always mischief-makers."

"But," said the cook, "when that housemaid of

ours asked you if that shawl was a gift, you said, '*Not exactly.*'"

"Did I?" said the woman. "I remember her often talking of the shawl, and I remember her saying that some rich person must have given the shawl to me; perhaps I answered, 'Not exactly,' to that. For my dear godmother was not rich; and it came to me by will."

Then the cook told this young woman of the injury the curious housemaid had done her; and when her mistress came in, she asked to see her, and she told her all the story, and finished by saying, that the young woman was now so poor that she had come to the town to sell the things that the housemaid had seen, and that the lady might see them herself, and hear the truth about them.

The lady took the woman again into her service; and proved her to be, what she had in fact always been, a good servant and an excellent Catholic.

The housemaid's ending was not so good. She had lost her place on account of her curiosity. She had got another place, and she had lost that through the same fault. A third place was lost for the same reason. No one can wonder at this; so troublesome a fault is not to be borne in a house. She had let the children's white mice out of a cage because she wanted to look at them. She had greased a beautiful dinner-dress, because she would open the wardrobe, where a lady visiting in the house had hung it, and show it to a fellow-servant; and then, in their hurry, some drops from the candle had fallen on it. She had opened a box that shut with a spring, and not knowing how the spring acted, she had forced down the cover, and broken it; and it was a very valuable box, and could never be repaired. She had opened and dirtied books, and injured paintings. At last, from never trying to correct this fault, she got so mean and dishonourable, that she would listen to conversations not intended for her to hear; and she had been seen reading a letter left on the table. No one would have any thing to do with her. To conceal her fault, she often told falsehoods. People get from bad to worse, as you know; and when last she was heard of, she was in lodgings, getting a very uncertain living by going out to work by the day; every body said she was not a person fit for such an honourable state of life as that of a good and trusted servant.

This young woman was always saying that curiosity was no great sin, after all. But we must not excuse ourselves in this way. It is the part of a Catholic to adorn the Church of Christ. When a good Catholic observes in herself a constantly-recurring little fault, she will not say, "Oh, it is a little fault, I need not trouble to break myself of it!" You know that a good Catholic will not say that; and you know what she will say. She will say it is a small fault, therefore it will be easy to correct it; and if it looks small to her mind and yet is difficult to cure, then she will be afraid of this fault's strength, and very earnestly try to cure it; for she will think of its consequences both to her neighbour and herself. Remember this, if you are ever tempted to give way to curiosity.

A curious person is never fit to be trusted. If a

girl has yielded herself up captive to this vice, she ought never to expect to be called trustworthy. This is a true story of a young woman, who might have been a good and valued servant if she had not been curious.

A gentleman had been staying in Germany: he was a learned man, and knew a great deal about animals and insects, and all living creatures. In Germany there is a beautiful and an extraordinary frog. It does not live on the ground as other frogs do, but in trees. Its colour is a lovely bright green; and it hops from twig to twig, looking more like a leaf endowed with life than a frog. Up in the trees, on the highest branches, when the weather is fine, these little green creatures frolic about, living on insects, and glittering bright green in the warm clear sunlight.

The peasants in Germany catch these small green frogs, and put them in bottles—in white glass bottles which you can see through. Into the bottle they put a little ladder, and then they tie something over the top which will be sufficient to keep the frog safe in the bottle, and which yet will give him air enough to breathe. I am afraid the pretty little green frog cannot like this life very much. The bottle must be but a small world for one accustomed to live in the sun and air so freely, and the ladder must be but a bad exchange for the branching trees, where he has skipped and hopped about so happily.

But the German peasant has a reason for putting the green frog in a bottle. He wants to know what the weather will be, that he may manage his crops and do his out-door work safely. And, wonderful to say, in bad weather the frog stays at the bottom of the bottle; and as the weather improves, the frog mounts the steps of the little ladder, and in really fine weather he is found quite up at the top. Now this learned gentleman, who had been to Germany, had succeeded in bringing some of these frogs alive and well all the way to England. The day after he got home, a curious housemaid, longing to know what was in the glass in which they had travelled, opened it. The frogs croaked; she threw the glass down,—they hopped out of the window into the garden, and there it was supposed that a duck had eaten them, for they were never seen again.

Do you think that such a girl as that was worth keeping? Was she trustworthy? Try hard to restrain curiosity. It is a mean troublesome vice. When once young people have given way to curiosity, they find the temptations to it come often and very strong. Curiosity leads people into real sin very often. That liking to know about things of which they had better be ignorant; that curious inquiring into the particulars of acts that ought not to have been committed,—is wrong, and dangerous to the soul, and is one way of tempting the soul to sin; and these are the ways that curious people get into. Curiosity is difficult to cure when people have long given way to it; but like all other evils, it is easy to cure in the beginning. Examine your hearts, and keep a watch over yourselves. If you feel curious, determine never to indulge yourself in thinking on the subject that has excited your curiosity. If gossiping people offer to tell you things which your own curious heart would like to know about, have the courage to say that such things do not concern you, and refuse to hear. Curiosity is soon killed if treated in this way. And in this way all good, well-taught women will act.

"I am curious; I am sure that I have very often been too curious," said Jane Isles. "I never thought of the meanness and the mischief of this vice before."

Tears came into the young girl's eyes. There was no merry laugh on Jane's lips now.

"Stop, stop, Jane," said Anne Wilton; "you are not the only curious girl among us,—I too am guilty. I can remember so many times when I have been guilty of improper curiosity. I am glad and thankful to have had the knowledge of this fault brought home to me before I went into service. Oh, Mrs. Maitland, we shall often think of you."

"Think of me, and pray for me," said the lady. "I was carefully instructed, and taken as great care of as a child. I have seen much of the world. I give you a little of my experience; and if in return you will remember me, and pray for me, then we shall have helped each other."

CHAPTER VIII.

COURAGE, PRESENCE OF MIND, AND RECOLLECTION.

PERHAPS, as we read the heading of this chapter, some of us may think that, as these instructions were given chiefly for the pleasure and benefit of girls and young women, courage might have been left out. Courage, perhaps, is thought to be a manly virtue; if so, what have girls to do with courage? It is natural to women to be timid.

"Yes," Mrs. Maitland said, "it *is* natural to women to be timid, and on that very account we are now going to consider the great value of courage. Women are very often placed in positions where it is well for them to possess that true courage which forms one part of a Christian's character; for the best courage a woman can have will be found to be that strong, firm, quiet courage which arises from a true, unwavering trust in God; and which is a practical knowledge of His being Father, Friend, and Protector in a more powerful sense than any tongue can tell, and in a way that only the Christian heart can truly feel. The Lord is the helper and protector of all those who love and fear Him. And all that fear the Lord are blessed, both little and great.

But there is a nervousness which often troubles good people. They are frightened and made ill in themselves, and useless to their neighbours, before they have time to remember that God sees them, and that their guardian angel is by their side. There is no doubt that, except in cases of sickness, all these sudden nervous feelings may be overcome by *trying* to overcome them. Of course this victory is most easily won by those persons who begin early. And it is so very desirable to overcome such distressing feelings, that it is to be hoped that all of you who read or hear this will learn courage yourselves, and help your friends to learn it.

For a person to be really frightened is a dreadful and dangerous thing. But persons who have early accustomed themselves to trust in God, to think of their guardian angel, and to lift up their hearts in prayer when in any alarm, will never be dreadfully and dangerously frightened. They are full of a Christian courage, and are not going to be afraid. But, remember, that whoever frightens another is a contemptible coward; and often ends in being worse than a coward—in being a mischief-maker and a sinner.

Only a short time since, a party of young girls were walking on a road near the town of Preston in Lancashire. To their surprise, they saw a coffin in the road; they advanced towards it, when, all at once, without any one touching it, the coffin in the road began to move. The girl nearest to it felt a sudden fright. The other girls ran away; then, I believe, she ran away too. The girl went home, and felt rather ill; the next day she died. They found out how the coffin moved. Some boys had been carrying it. When these boys saw the girls coming, one of them thought he would frighten them; so he tied a string to the coffin-handle, and jumped over the fence out of sight. As the girls came up, he pulled the string, and made the coffin move; the consequence was, that all the girls were frightened, and that one died. For she really did die of the fright; her body was opened, to find out the cause of her death, and the surgeon described how the shock had caused a sudden overflow of bile, and the bursting of an inward part, and this, the day following the fright, caused her death.

Many such stories might be told. I could tell you how a child suddenly became an idiot from a fright which some playfellows had shamefully contrived. But such stories are too sad and too disagreeable to tell. The facts are mentioned here to put you on your guard against ever frightening any body. You don't know what mischief you may do, or what evil may arise out of your wicked folly.

It often happens to people to be by themselves under very trying circumstances, when great courage is required; and I can only repeat, that no courage can be thoroughly depended upon that does not arise from trust in God,—trust in God, which is a knowledge of God's love to us, and an appeal from our poor love to His, which is all-powerful;—trust in God is the foundation of the only courage that will never fail, and that is always ready for use.

An anecdote of a little girl will please you here. There was a child who frequently had to go from the house where her mother lived to a town not far off. She walked with a servant-girl or a friend, and the way they went was by a wall, within which was chained so fierce a dog that he was the terror of the neighbourhood. The police had been spoken to about this dog. He had once broken his chain, and had nearly injured the passersby; but as no one had as yet been really hurt, the owners of the dog thought they had a right to keep him there for the protection of their property. When the servant-maid, or the friend with whom the child walked, was almost powerless with fright, the dog barking and leaping, so that they heard the rattling of his chain as he flung himself against the wall in his efforts to get at them, the little child would press her fingers tightly round the hand of her companion, and walking steadily forward, lead her past the danger. They knew by the pressure of her fingers, and sometimes by the trembling of her hand, and her pale face, that the child felt fear; but her courage always conquered. She never hesitated. And at last many people said that the only person in the neighbourhood who dared to walk steadily past that wall was this small child. It was her mother who found out what the child did to keep her little heart so strong. As soon as she came to the wall, she said, "Holy Mary, Mother of God, pray for us sinners *now*;" then walking on, she said, " now—*now*—NOW,"—by this time she had nearly passed the wall,—" now, and at the hour of our death: Amen." And so the danger was got over. That child knew a great deal about Christian courage, and the true strength of trust in God.

You will like to hear that representations were at last made to the magistrates about this dog, and the neighbourhood was relieved of its dangerous presence.

But there is a false courage, a sort of foolish or ignorant recklessness: you must not mistake false courage for true. Like every other feeling, you can find out if it be true or false by inquiring how much religion is in it. You shall have instances of true courage and false. In a bad neighbourhood—in a wicked town—many evil-living people dwelt. There lay in this place, dying, a poor girl—she was dying without religion; no priest, no Sacraments. She was not wicked, like many who were around her; she was a French girl, and could not speak English; and if she asked for a priest, no one understood her. The news of what was happening got about. Girls from another part of the town went boldly through the danger of bad company, and bad sounds and sights, just to see her,—to know what she was like—to hear her queer talk—to wonder where she came from and who she belonged to. Their mothers and friends said, "Don't go; there are thieves, drunkards, swearers, people of all kinds of evil lives, there; don't you." The girls said they were not afraid. Was that a true courage? How much religion was there in their actions? None. They were not courageous. They were bold in a bad way. They ran a great risk of seeing and hearing sin, and of offending God. There was no true courage in them. There was a bad, daring spirit,—a spirit that forgot God; and such young women, in any circumstances of real terror, would certainly be cowards: there are no such cowards in trouble as those who forget God. But, by the merciful providence of God, there happened to be in the neighbourhood of the dying French girl a good woman; and when she saw her, she said that she would fetch the priest. Then all the wicked people said that they would have no priest there; that she should not go; they even threatened her with many evils, and some said that they would take her life if she went. But the woman thought within herself that she ought not to be afraid, and she went.

Was that true courage? Yes; it was trust in God. The foolish girls who risked their characters in bad company had only trusted in themselves; but this woman's trust was in God, and her courage was great and good. And she was allowed to perform the good action of bringing the priest to the dying, and the God she served preserved her in safety.

You may be sure of this, that Satan loves to see people act on a false courage,—to hear people say they are not afraid when they ought to be afraid; to see people trust in themselves, and forget the commands of God. There is no real courage in being bold to sin, or to run your soul into danger; it is being vain and foolhardy, and not courageous.

Neither is there any true courage in running great risks when prudent people would avoid risk. If you are *obliged*, if it is ever *your duty*, to walk at night in a lonely place, by an unfrequented road, do it courageously, trusting in God. But you need not run risks, and do from wilfulness or a foolish boldness what prudent people avoid doing; there is no courage in that. Such a distinction you can make for yourselves under other and various circumstances. Some foolish servants leave doors open and windows unbolted, even at night, in their master's house, and think it very grand to say they are not afraid. But all that is mere folly; they have no right to run risks, or to throw temptations in people's way. Some persons are so very ignorant as to make a boast of this recklessness, which they wrongly call courage. They talk of fire and of gunpowder, and say, Oh, they are not afraid; they leave the most dangerous thing in the world about, even in the way of children, and laugh at prudence.

Of course you see that such conduct is not courage, but only ignorance,—an ignorance of which you, who have had the advantage of being at school and of having your minds informed, will never be guilty. To know when to be cautious and when to be bold, is to be educated on these points; it is the ignorant who are rash, and blindly daring, and fond of running risks.

We will now leave the subject of Courage for a short time; but we will come back to it before we close this chapter. We will now think about *Presence of Mind*.

It is a thing worthy of remark, that all holy persons, as far as we can learn from the Lives of the Saints and other histories, have all been possessed of this virtue; and if we look about for ourselves, and think of those persons who have seemed to us to be among the holiest people known to us, I think we shall say that they all possess presence of mind.

Now, as true courage, particularly a woman's true courage,—for women are not naturally courageous,—as, then, true courage is allied to trust in God, so true presence of mind is allied to the abiding habitual sense of the presence of God. People who habitually remember the presence of God are not frightened out of their own presence of mind; and so the holier people are, the less liable they will be to lose presence of mind; and they will be more likely to preserve steadiness of nerve, and composure of spirit, and wisdom in judgment, than other people.

Presence of mind is of incalculable value to persons living in the world. Sudden things happen,—sudden joys, sudden losses, sudden gains, sudden accidents. People have been known to go mad from joy, and never to recover their senses. They might have been very good people; but if their friends and teachers had helped them in early life to preserve that sense of God's presence which is part of the education of every Catholic child, and which no Catholic ought ever to allow herself to lose, I think in their sudden joy they would have kept their senses.

It is hardly necessary to repeat, that presence of mind is of incalculable advantage to persons living in the world. We may consider presence of mind as the power of quickly bringing into use any knowledge you may have acquired when such knowledge is wanted. For instance, we have all of us lighted a match very often. It is a very simple thing to do, and requires but a small amount of knowledge. We have also observed, when lighting either a match of wood or a piece of folded paper, that if we hold the match with the flame downward, it lights quickly, the flame running up the paper or wood to our fingers, and burning the paper as it rises. We know also that when lighted, if we hold it with the flame upwards, like a candle, it will burn steadily and well for a sufficient time, that is, for the time required to use it; and we know that if we hold the paper or wood sideways, or in the same position in which the match would be if we placed it lying on the ground, that the flame will go out. If you drop a lighted match inside the fender on the hearth, it goes out in its lying posture almost directly, without consuming what remains of the match. All this you may not think of when you light a candle; but you have the knowledge, and from habit and experience you act upon it.

Now if you came into a room and saw a girl on fire, it would be a good act of presence of mind to bring this knowledge quickly into practice, without letting the fright and horror of the sad sight overcome your reason. It would be an act of presence of mind for you to cry out, "Lie down! lie down!" It would, on the part of the unhappy girl whose clothes were on fire, be an act of presence of mind to obey you. If she lies down, the flames will subside in a great degree of their own accord. Now another act of presence of mind on your part would be to close the door, because the admission of air feeds fire, as you know by the use of the bellows, or by opening a window to get up the fire in the grate. You also know that fire can be suffocated; though coal burns so fast and well as to be used for making a fire, yet if you throw on too much, you can put a fire out with the very material that makes it. It would, then, be another act of presence of mind on your part to suffocate the fire, that will otherwise cause the death of the sufferer we have been thinking of. If she is on the floor, the rug, carpet, table-cover, any clothes in the room,—your own shawl, if you have one on,—the door-mat, if it is not straw,—may, any or all of them, be used to suffocate the flames. As she lies, throw them on her, press them close to her; if she has presence of mind, she will help to roll herself in any thing she can lay hold of for the purpose, always remembering to stir the air with her arms as little as possible. By this means life will be saved and great injury prevented. There is no case in which presence of mind is of more use than in cases of fire.

But it is also of great use in accidents. If a child has fallen and broken its leg, a mother or nurse, acting from affection, and *without* presence of mind, will immediately take up the child in her arms. The leg hanging down gives horrible pain; and if they are awkward, the broken bone is forced through the skin. This is called a compound fracture; and through the want of that presence of mind that would have found out how the child was hurt before they moved it, and that would then have had it carried as nearly in the same posture in which they found it as possible on a board or a shutter, they have injured the child, possibly for life, and given it all the danger and distress of a painful operation.

A true story of extraordinary presence of mind will interest you here. A soldier, called John Hall, was in India with his regiment. The regiment was at Madras. John was a clever, strong-minded man, and gifted with great presence of mind, as you will hear; but John was often in disgrace, because he was a drunkard. In consequence of this fault, he was once sentenced to a few days of solitary confinement. He was confined in a cell built against a rock. Here he had his bedding; and always before lying down for the night he had to stop up an air-hole which was placed in the side of the wall, almost close to the ground, for ventilation. One night John Hall forgot to do this. It was dark. He was lying down, and alone; he was, however, awake, and he heard a rustling in the cell close by him. He guessed what it was; and he was quite right. He guessed that one of the great Indian snakes had got into the cell through the unstopped air-hole; and he felt the snake begin at his foot and crawl over it. The creature he felt was of enormous size. It had got under the bed-clothes; and it came up on his body, over his chest, and even stretched itself across his face. With the greatest presence of mind, John never moved. His knowledge of the habits of these great Indian snakes came quickly to his use; he knew they were easily provoked by even a touch to bite, but that they would often only bite in self-defence, and that the best way to show the serpent that there was no need for self-defence was to lie as still as if he was dead. So the great serpent, which was quite as long as John was tall, writhed its cold slimy body up and down, and round and about this man's body, and backwards and forwards on his face, and he never moved a muscle all the time; and this moving about of the reptile occupied an hour. You may suppose how long an hour seemed under such circumstances. At last the snake coiled itself up close by the side of John's head, and went to sleep.

Flat on his back, with this snake sleeping close to his ear and leaning against him, did John lie without moving till daybreak. During the darkness the snake had managed to get under John's pillow. When the light came, the man looked round. He saw a large stone on the further side of his cell, and with the greatest care rolled himself off his pillow, and got to where this great stone lay; then, armed with the stone, and seeing by the increasing light where his enemy had got, he knelt on the pillow, yet left room for the snake to put out his head; and then, confining the creature's body by the pillow, he killed him with the stone. When John's breakfast was brought, he and the dead snake were found together. The snake was then discovered to be one of the most venomous known, whose bite is always and speedily mortal. John Hall had saved his life by his presence of mind. The natives of the country all agreed in saying that John had acted in the best possible way to avoid death; but there are very few persons in the world who could have sustained so great a trial through the darkness of a whole night. He was freed from his confinement as a reward for his courage and ready presence of mind.

If all Christians can acquire presence of mind, then all who are going out to get their living in the world ought to try very hard to acquire it. Try by prayer and by practice.

And this mention of *practice*—the trying to practise the virtues which you desire to possess, and for which you pray—brings us to think of the other virtue mentioned in the heading of this chapter, namely, Recollection.

Recollection here does not mean mere memory, but *a state of mind.*

Suppose you were in some place where, for a time

at least, there were a great many things to be done, and where your master or mistress might call you at any moment to do this or that, you did not know in what order, or at what time. You would keep yourself in a state of mind fit for the difficult and important duties expected of you. You would not be in a state of hurry, and bustle, and nervousness, as if you had lost your head,—you would be full of recollectedness. Like a person plaiting a wide plait with a great many cords, you would keep all your cords in hand, manage them without confusion, and make a perfect and beautiful plait of a piece of work which many an ignorant looker-on might have thought a very confused-looking affair. Did you ever see any one making lace? Perhaps some who read this book can make lace themselves. Scores, perhaps hundreds, of threads, all pinned on a cushion, and some hanging on one side, some on the other, some in front. Some few rather coarser than others; a great many so fine, that the looker-on trembles lest there should ever be a knot, and has no idea how a thread could ever be fastened together again if it broke.

Then the girl who understands the work comes. Click, click go the beads and tassels that act as weights on the threads. All her ten fingers are moving. The threads are flung over and under, behind and before; the pins are pulled out and stuck in; and those who are watching think that such a wonderful confusion and puzzle of pins, and fingers, and threads, was never before seen in the world. All this while the girl, who is doing some really difficult pattern, has her eye on her cushion. All the talk about her does not distract her mind a moment. Not one wrong movement is made. Of all those threads that look so confused, not one goes wrong. Every pin is stuck in its right place, and the pattern is formed perfectly, and the lace grows on the cushion as we look, and is a lovely and wonderful work.

Now this girl has learnt to do her work, and has taken pains to learn. And yet, now that she is doing it, it is not a mere act of memory—the pattern is too difficult for that; and yet it is a sort of memory, only not exactly that sort of memory which enables you to say the pence-table, or the multiplication-table, without thinking at all about it. She, as the pattern is very difficult, uses her memory, that is true; but she thinks too —she is in a state of recollectedness. You will observe here that she has *presence of mind* also. She must not be in a state to be disturbed and distracted. And she must have courage; for such a pattern as I have supposed is a very difficult pattern—so difficult, that many cowardly girls would have said: "Oh, I shall never learn that; oh, I am afraid of the trouble; oh, I have no courage to try."

And this last mention of courage brings us back to courage again.

You must try to acquire a good moral courage—a courage which shall give you strength to try to do every duty that belongs to your state, or that it is desirable for you to undertake. A courage also that shall make you strong to avoid evil. Thousands are *persuaded* into little sins, or at least into actions that had better be left undone. Moral courage will enable you to say 'No' when you ought to say 'No.' It often requires great courage to say that little word, and to act it bravely out. It is so easy to go with the multitude to do evil. The downward road is wide and smooth, and looks pleasant. Crowds of merry hearts and happy faces, as it may seem to you, are going that way; it may be very hard to say 'No.' Perhaps these people, who seem to you so merry and happy, never go to confession; or perhaps they intend to go next Easter, and are ready to say they are half sorry they did not go last Easter; that they are not so bad; they are still Catholics in their hearts; they are too light-hearted to trouble. Don't believe in their light-heartedness. Rather believe that they have not had the courage to do right, to avoid temptation, and to serve God with a steady mind. Keep to your own firm, courageous way. There is more joy in loving God than in forgetting Him. There is more comfort in one act of faith before the Blessed Sacrament than in any companionship you can have with those who have not courage to own Him before men. And now, to return to presence of mind: there is a moral sense in which it is extremely valuable to Christians, and particularly to Christian girls.

It requires courage to say '*No*' at the proper time very often. But it requires great presence of mind not to say '*Yes*' before you have thought. It is so natural to all amiable persons to oblige, that many a good girl has been first taken into bad company, just because she had not sufficient presence of mind to consider her answer to a dangerous invitation before she gave it. And then having said '*Yes*' when she ought to have said '*No*,' she had not courage to say she had changed her mind, and refuse to go.

Good girls don't go into dangerous company of their own free-will and with knowledge. So, presence of mind to discover what things really are, so that the soul may not be injured unawares, is most necessary to Catholic girls. And with courage and presence of mind, acquire recollection. Think once more of the composed, earnest, instructed, and undistracted state of mind of the lace-maker. She is managing a hundred troublesome little threads; and you must manage a hundred little trials, making out of them the beautiful whole of a Christian life.

Some girls who go into busy places to get their living say, that they "pass so many things through their hands and heads in the day, that they have no time to think of their souls; no time to examine their conscience; no time to think of God;" and so neglect the Sacraments.

If they had learnt the meaning of recollection, and gained a habit of recollectedness, they would never say that. They would so manage the hundred things they have to do, that every one should be done to the glory of God. By courage, presence of mind, and recollectedness, they would still have Him in all their thoughts, and do all their works to His honour.

It is sad to hear it said that some good girls, who lead holy lives, and keep close to our Blessed Lord by prayer and a diligent frequenting of the Sacraments, are not as perfect in their worldly work as they ought to be. This is nothing less than a disgrace. It is a disgrace that all of us must try never to bring on ourselves and on holy Church.

Perhaps this consideration may help us to do better. Our Blessed Lord, when He was born of the Blessed Virgin, chose the position in life of a working-man. He chose to pass for the carpenter's son, and through the youth which He condescended to spend in the home of His immaculate Mother in Nazareth, He chose to be subject to her and to St. Joseph.

Now let all of us who have active labour to perform in this world, all who have chosen to serve others, all who are engaged doing service at home, on our knees, think sometimes of this awful and wonderful time of the life of our Blessed Lord and God.

What kind of service was there in the holy home at Nazareth? Think for a moment of this. What a dignity it gives to all service! What a holy thing work becomes! Is it christianlike to do that in a slovenly way which our Blessed Lady, and great St. Joseph, and God Himself, set us the example of doing? We can all of us save our souls in our work, and do our work so well at the same time as to reflect credit on our mother —the Church. Courage, presence of mind, and recollection, we must try to gain by the blessing of God; they will keep us from evil, and help us to great good.

This afternoon's instruction seemed to Mary Hardy to be the most interesting of all that they had listened to. She was a very good, sensible, thoughtful girl, and she enjoyed having ideas presented to her in a practical way. After she had been two years in service, in a rather difficult place, she told Jane and Anne that courage, presence of mind, and recollection had been her best friends; and that the remembrance of these instructions had often kept her from misery, and filled her with hope.

CHAPTER IX.

MODESTY.

"GIVE me your best attention, dear girls, while we speak about Modesty," said Mrs. Maitland.

Acts of immodesty are sinful. Whether committed by men or women, they belong to that horrible class of sin of which to speak among good Christians is a shame. We are not going to think of gross sins here, nor even of those smaller crimes which are the beginnings of evil, and which are contrary to good morals and injurious to the soul. As Christian women, you will avoid every thing of this kind, and all company that may be suspected of a want of proper strictness on this subject. If you ever have cause to suspect or fear that you have got into company not strictly modest, you must fly. Don't think that you can stay and conquer temptation, that you can remain and get the pleasure and not be worse for the danger; that thought is wrong, and that hope is a false one. The thought and the hope are themselves the temptations of the devil, in order to keep you where you ought not to be. You must not stay; your safety is in flight. You are in the wrong place, and you must get out of it as fast as you can, and with as few words as possible.

There are many places of amusement to which girls

might go, if they were properly managed. But it is certain, unhappily, that, in this country particularly, many amusements are managed so improperly that all good girls are better away.

There is no harm in going to a concert. Music is a delightful amusement, and one that a good Christian may reasonably enjoy. But immodest songs are sung very often at cheap concerts, and this must prevent your going to them. It is better never to hear a song again as long as you live, than to defile your mind and pollute your soul with words which suggest sin and do the work of Satan. It is an insult to a virtuous, modest girl to say or to sing immodest words in her presence. Where there is any chance of such insults being offered, there good young women will not like to go.

There are public gardens which are very pleasant to visit and very beautiful to look at, and where foreign birds and animals, and beautiful trees and sweet flowers, are pleasant to the eye, and may be very instructive to the mind. But there are times when such places are thrown open to the public at cheap prices, when games of an immodest sort are played there. It seems sad to say it,—indeed, it really is a very sad thought,—but modest girls cannot go at these times. But for the immodesty of other people, they might go and enjoy themselves honestly; but into danger good Catholic girls must never go. They must not have their names mixed up with the names of those who do evil; they had better avoid the sight of bold romps and liberty-taking plays, which are contrary to the dignity of a Christian woman's character. All this kind of thing is hurtful to true modesty, and to holy delicacy of feeling. It might be a dangerous excitement to go, and a dreadful kind of pleasure; but to stay at home for the love of our Blessed Lord is best and sweetest; and when you come to die, you will be glad that you chose the company of the Immaculate Virgin, and that of your bright angel guardian, and of purified Saints, rather than the company of those whose words and actions are gross, and their example dangerous. If you observe a proper care in choosing your companions and your pleasures, you will be sure to show a proper modesty in your own behaviour.

It is perhaps natural to young women to love praise and to like being admired. But let us try to *deserve* praise and to be *worthy* of admiration. Those who love praise and admiration, and who do not turn their thoughts inward, and try to be worthy of the approbation of Him from whom no secrets are hid, are sure to grow insincere and pretending. There is no modesty in pretending to be what we are not. Modesty is always sincere and truthful. There is modesty in manner, in appearance, in little actions, even in voice and in words.

A truly modest person has no conceited ways with her, no flinging about of the hands or arms, or tossings of the head; none of those little ways which you have often heard described as "saucy manners." A truly modest person will not wear extraordinary clothes, will not try to be the very first to put on a new fashion, or to be in any extreme of dress.

A truly modest person will not talk loud, or go about singing her own songs or tunes to the distraction of other people. She will not contradict or interrupt old people when they are talking, or be uncivil to the poor, or contemptuous to the ignorant, or rude and dictatorial to children, or act proudly towards persons beneath her, or impertinently to those who are above her.

A modest person will never try to attract attention; indeed, she will naturally do things in a way which will never draw observers. She will walk neither too slow nor too fast, but just naturally, according to time and circumstances. When she speaks to people, she will not make a loud fuss or a conceited ceremony of it; but all will be done, without pretence, in a natural, sincere, modest manner.

This is the description of the manners of a Christian girl. Do you think that such perfect manners are only expected of *ladies?* You are quite mistaken if you think so. Such manners are expected of *you*—of *you*, not because you are to pretend to be a lady,—for our positions in life, whatever they may be, are such as God has ordered,—but because you are a Christian girl. Good manners are very pleasant; and the best manners known are the modest manners of a Christian. Such pleasing ways are expected of you; for St. Paul said this: "Let your modesty be known unto all men." And this also is in Holy Scripture, which is the written Word of God: "Put ye on therefore, as the elect of God, holy and beloved, modesty." And this also in the Proverbs: "The end of modesty is the fear of the Lord, riches, and glory, and life."

You will find out easily, from what has been said of modesty, that modest persons are not great talkers; that they probably love silence, as a comfort and refreshment to their modest souls. It is modest to be "swift to hear, and slow to speak."

It is modest not to be too obstinate in your opinion, for the best have been deceived sometimes. It is modest to distrust your own judgment, for other persons may have had surer means of knowing the truth than yourself. It is modest to receive blame for any fault without resentment. It is modest to be ready to learn of those who may be in many things more ignorant than you are.

But there is no modesty in keeping silence when you *ought* to speak, or letting wrong things be done when you could easily prevent them by a proper interference. If in your presence any thing contrary to propriety is said, you must be bold enough to speak, and put a stop at once to all license of tongue. No modest girl will ever allow the smallest license of manner. Of course she will never, by word or action, tempt any man to take a liberty with her. Many a joke has ended in terrible earnest; and there are very few girls in the world who have not had warnings enough of the great dangers that often grow out of slight beginnings.

A flighty girl—a girl who by her words and manners, by her free jokes and bold boastings, attracts men to dispute, threaten, laugh at, or take liberties with her—is a misfortune to her neighbourhood. The temptations she flings in people's way, the evil thoughts to which she encourages people, the scandal she gives, the danger that she becomes to her companions,—are all misfortunes of a most serious kind. Her ways are the ways of the wicked, and all modest girls will do well to avoid her.

Perhaps many people admire her, and say she is gay and pleasant, and good company. No doubt she attracts a great deal of notice, and for a time she seems to be very popular and to have influence, and she draws others to imitate her. But it is the sort of interest and the sort of admiration that no modest Christian girl can look upon except with horror. She has neither the modest mind nor modest manners which we have just read of. She does all those things to attract attention that a modest girl avoids doing. There are better things than the admiration given to the vain and flighty girl: the love of God, the happiness and strength that grows out of the abiding recollection of living in His presence, the approval of the good, the approbation of the wise, the blessings of thankful friends and happy parents, and the feeling in your own conscience that you are trying to serve God, and the joy of your own heart learning to love God, and the faith by which you persevere,—these solid, undying consolations and joys are the best things we can know upon earth; and the soul cannot be satisfied with any thing less. Pray frequently and with fervour to our Blessed Lady and St. Joseph to preserve your modesty. Meditate on the fact of God having chosen an immaculate Virgin for His Mother, and of His having committed her to the care of her most chaste spouse Saint Joseph. Make them the frequent companions of your thoughts, and you are not likely to go wrong.

If you are ever in so responsible a position as to be

placed in authority over others, be very careful to preserve an example of modesty, and to check the smallest deviation from a strict propriety in good time. Don't be afraid of being thought strict. It is good to be strict, and respectable too; even the world acknowledges this. The best characters like a strict house best. There is no getting on properly without discipline. So don't be afraid of being justly strict to others. Only pray diligently to be able to judge yourself with severity, and ask daily for grace and strength to perform your duties to your own soul. Those who go to the Sacraments regularly, and keep the closest watch over themselves, are the best able to take care of others.

If you have the care of children, guard their modesty carefully. Never allow a coarse word or action in their presence.

If you have the care of a sick person, be modest in your treatment; and careful in all your actions to preserve that delicacy and respect towards the sick person that true modesty demands. Sometimes, if a nurse has the care of a person in a state of insensibility, if she is a coarse, immodest-minded woman, she does not care what she says before the sufferer, or how she treats her. This is quite wrong, for there should be no failing in modesty of conduct, even when alone; and it is unfeeling also, for what we call a state of insensibility is not always one of unconsciousness. People on recovery have repeated all that has been said before them. And even if no one understood, God and His holy Angels see and hear.

And should you ever have any thing to do with the

dead, be modest. A great respect is owing to those bodies of Christians that are to be raised up at the last day, incorruptible and full of glory, to live for ever in heaven. They have been the temples of the Holy Ghost. God Himself, in the Blessed Sacrament, has visited them often. Be respectful, therefore, and modest in your treatment of the dead.

In all your ways, in speaking and laughing, in dress and manners, in movements and actions, pray to our Lord Jesus Christ for grace to exhibit a perfect modesty. This is the advice of a holy priest; and he says also, that modesty obtains a good name for ourselves, and augments the glory of God. Pray, then, for grace to obtain this virtue, and to practise it diligently.

Quietly and thoughtfully the girls went home that night; for they felt a sort of awe as they walked through the streets of the great town in which they lived, and recalled the instructions they had received, and remembered what their holy books said of the sweet virtue of modesty. They shook hands with each other kindly when they came to the street where they had to take separate ways. They had been more silent than usual; but their hearts were full of good thoughts and pious resolutions. When they said their night prayers, they asked strength of God to keep pure and good in thought, word, and deed; and commended themselves with fervour to His holy Mother.

CHAPTER X.

TEMPERANCE AND SOBRIETY.

"Do you think that Temperance means not getting drunk only?" asked Mrs. Maitland.

No; we must make that word mean more than that. But first, it may be taken in that sense. Now it is a terrible and melancholy fact, that great numbers of women drink—drink to drunkenness. Sad as this is, it is true, and many of you young and innocent women, who are interesting yourselves in this book, have seen women drunk, and know how miserable and degraded those unhappy creatures become who are victims of the vile vice of intemperance.

These poor wretches were not always drunkards. Once they were young and innocent as you are. How did they get into this bad state of mortal sin?

If you ask this question, you will always get the same sort of answer, and this is it.

"It was company—always so fond of company; they would go with any one for the sake of company, so often with the wrong sort of people; but she must have company—the love of company led her away."

That is the sort of answer that has been given thousands of times, when people have asked how it was that a woman could so fall away.

This helps us to another meaning of the word 'temperance.' The poor drunkard was intemperately fond of pleasure. If she had been temperate in her pleasures, she might never have learnt to drink. And so temperance means the moderate enjoyment of lawful pleasures; and we must therefore be temperate not only in drinking, but in eating, and in every other enjoyment which is pleasant to the body, and may, by indulgence, be turned into an injury to the soul.

Bessey Brown was very fond of company. From a child, wherever people were gathered together, there was Bessey. For this she would leave work and duty. She would forget that she was earning her living, forget that a sick mother wanted her in the house. If there was a fiddler in the street, or a singer, or Italian boys with a monkey, down went Bessey's embroidery-frame, and she went off to where the idle crowd was gathering, losing her time, when, to her, time was money. She was inordinately fond of company, she was not temperate in the enjoyment of society. Scoldings at home for this fault made her dislike home. Good girls, too, reproached her. Why did she neglect her mother? Why had she done so little work? Why had she earned so little money? Why was she not clean and neat, like the other girls who worked as she did? All this vexed her. She knew she was wrong, but she was too fond of her wrong ways to try to change them.

As good girls reproached her, she got among companions who were less particular. They were merry girls too, and very fond of company. To plays and balls and concerts Bessey went now. And as she had not money to pay for admittance, she let wild youths "treat" her. And they gave her strong drink for refreshment, and often kept her out merry-making all night. Her conscience was often sore. But when she made an effort to be steady, her bad companions said, "Pay us back that money." And as she could not pay, she felt in bondage to their wishes, and often went out when she now would gladly have stayed at home.

Then one of these wild young men said he would marry her. And Bessey thought it would be a good thing to get away from home, and into a place of her own, and begin life over again. So she consented to be his wife. And she made some weak resolutions about leading a steady life.

The young man was not of any religion. He laughed at Bessey when she said she was a Catholic, and so Bessey never liked saying any thing more about religion. He said he was not going to a church to be married. So they were married at the register-office. Then for a week this man was drunk. He had never learnt any thing about temperance. It vexed Bessey. But she went at night to public-houses to get him home. Before their marriage her husband had treated Bessey to spirits, and now he would have her drink with him. Sometimes, just to get peace, she would drink; and sometimes to make herself forgetful of the things her conscience was reminding her of, and sometimes because they were feeling poor, and she had scarcely eaten any thing all day, and she was glad to stop the cravings of hunger with gin.

No more Mass; no more acts of love to God. No

more contrition, nor confession, nor any good resolutions, nor purposes of amendment, now. No more prayers. No more kneeling before the Crucifix; no more Christianity. For Bessey is now worse than a poor heathen who has never known the true religion. She has turned wilfully away from our blessed Lord, and chosen to serve Satan.

She still seeks company. Any thing, as she says, for a little happiness. True happiness she never knows. But riotous nights, with drinking and blasphemy, are better than the company of her own ruined heart and sinking soul. Her mother dies. And Bessey and her husband are both drunk after the funeral. A baby is born, and Bessey takes it to the priest to be christened. The priest asks Bessey if she is a Catholic. She says, "Yes." How dreadful this is! The priest asks when she was last at her duties; she forgets. Was she at her duties last Easter? "No." The Easter before that? "No." When she was married? "No." Had she ever made her first communion? "Yes, oh, yes, at the Convent of the Sisters of Mercy." Oh, she was happy then. Oh, could those days come back again! Oh, how happy she should have been to have died after that first communion!—she wishes she had died. She sits down and cries. The priest still talks to her. He tells her she must come to confession, and that she must promise him to pray for grace to begin life all over again. But she says she never can tell how wicked she has been: how she loved company; how she went into any company, till none but the bad would have her. How then she heard blasphemies, and grew familiar with sin, and fond of riot, and amused with wickedness; and how her heart grew hard because she stilled its sorrows with drink, and stopped its fears with drink too. It is a sad story. But the priest encourages her, and says she has done one good action in bringing her child for baptism, that only by God's help could she have done that, and so God has not deserted her as she fears, but has had long-suffering patience towards her, and now waits to be gracious. Bessey promises to prepare for confession, and declares that she will try to lead a better life. But she has got among such a throng of people, there is always so much in and out, such constant company. And she has to fetch her husband home almost every night. He too is so fond of company. And he drinks with his companions. He ruins himself and starves her, all for the love of company, and to get drink.

Now she longs for quiet, and peace, and time to think of her soul. But she once cast peace away from her. She can't get it back again now.

The next thing the priest knew of Bessey he read in the column of the police-reports in the newspaper. Her husband had been brought before the magistrates. He had come home drunk, had quarrelled with her, knocked her down, trampled and stamped upon her. The other lodgers in the house had rushed into their room, and called "Murder!" When the police came in, the husband was taken into custody, and Bessey sent to the hospital.

The priest immediately went to see Bessey. She died of brain-fever, and never had her senses sufficiently to make the confession she had promised to make. Yet, at times, the priest thought she knew him, and he thought she seemed repentant. The man was sentenced to two years' hard labour. And the child was sent to the workhouse, to be brought up a Protestant.

That is the history of a Catholic girl who had never loved temperance. She could not go into company with temperance. She did not enjoy pleasure moderately. And this want of proper moderation led her into difficulties and temptations, and company of the worst sort, and into habits of sin which destroy the soul.

We may hope in this instance that this poor girl did repent. But her example should make all girls fear when they have longings after questionable indulgences; for they do not know into what dangers they may sink, if they once permit themselves an intemperate use of worldly enjoyments.

But perhaps some people may think that Bessey's is an extreme case, and that they should never sink as low as she did.

There are thousands of such cases as Bessey's. It is not an extreme case. Indeed, many are much worse; for many die without, as far as we know, any movement of the soul towards God at all.

But you may lose your soul, or greatly endanger its safety, and not behave with intemperance as shocking and open as Bessey's. You may, if you do not practise self-denial, and be temperate, lose your soul in quite *a respectable way*. Does this surprise you?

There was a laundress, a good woman with a good husband and good children. And she did her work well, and bore an excellent character; she had more work offered her, and then more, and more. She was not temperate. She thought she would make haste to get rich. She worked half the night and all the day. She was so busy with her washing-bills and her accounts, her reckoning and her receipts. The time she had given to examination of conscience, the few moments it had taken to say a prayer for the dead every day, the half-hour that used to be employed in hearing Mass on a day of devotion, were all given up. She had no time to hear her children's prayers, no leisure to speak of holy things to them. Not a moment, even on Sunday, to hear them say hymns and catechism. Poor woman, she was so intemperate in the enjoyment of money-making, that she was selling her soul for it. She had neither the heart to hire any one to help her, nor the courage to give up any of the work. She neglected her duties to her children, and she forgot her own soul. She had not been to confession for nearly a year, she had often neglected Mass, she had taken no care about the spiritual state of her children. Then suddenly she had a fit, and died without once showing any consciousness.

Now that is neither a life nor a death for a good Catholic girl to look forward to. All good girls must remember from this story, that if any earthly occupation or pleasure interferes with the soul, it must be given up, either entirely or in part, as the interest of the soul may require. You may be intemperate even in the pursuit of a good thing; for it was the duty of the laundress to help to support her family. And you are not to pursue any thing with such intemperate zeal as to risk your soul for its sake. A temperate mind is a peaceful mind. Great tempests of vices do not rage in a mind that is temperate. A holy tranquillity belongs to it. And as the temperate mind only enjoys this world's pleasures with moderation, it becomes filled with good desires. The good seed is not choked by the world in the soul given to temperance. The grace of God works surely where the desires of the flesh are subdued and kept within the bounds of temperance. Be then, not only not a drunkard, degrading your body, and bringing mortal sin upon your unhappy soul, but be temperate in all other pleasures of the senses. Do not be a glutton. A great many people eat more than is good for them. Many girls who have suffered poverty at home, if they get into better circumstances, grow too fond of eating, think too much about it, are too much disappointed if they are denied what they like. This is not being temperate. Remember how many there are who have to suffer hunger; and in that remembrance, eat what is good for you with thankfulness; and don't trouble after more than enough, or after things of extraordinary niceness. It is to some people a great victory when they have conquered the intemperate longing after good things to eat. Good Christians will try to obtain this victory from very high motives. They will remember the state of poverty which our Blessed Lord chose, and they will not pamper their bodies for His sake.

The Church by appointing fasts tells the Christian that to deny himself in food is good and right. Fasting expresses our desire to conquer the flesh, and make our fleshly desires obedient to the will, in order to bring our will in union with the will of God. Thus fasting is an act of devotion. And to all who would make fasting into an act of devotion, it will clearly be a duty to be at all times temperate.

Eat at regular times, and eat with a thankful appetite what is prepared for you. But don't let your appetite crave after little luxuries, don't let your thoughts dwell on eating, and don't get into the foolish habit of eating little bits and scraps all day long. Some people, particularly very young servants, can hardly keep themselves from taking scraps to eat whenever they have the opportunity. If they go into the larder, or the dairy, or open a cupboard, they must take something, however small. When they carry down dinner, when they bring up fruit or biscuits, they must just take a little bit. Of course this is foolish and dishonourable, often dirty, and always improper. But Christians have a high motive for never giving way to these suggestions of the taste. They desire to be temperate, because temperance is a Christian virtue. And they know that this virtue is to be practised on small occasions as well as on great ones. They have gained a victory over themselves, and they have their taste in subjection; the same motive that keeps them from drinking to excess, which is a great crime, will keep them from committing little faults, and failing in trifles. They are temperate both in eating and drinking, in great things and small.

Temperance is very good for the body as well as the soul. All over-indulgence is bad for the health. Every thing that pampers the body weakens it; and a pampered, indulged, and unconquered body brings a weight of dullness to the soul.

"He that is temperate shall prolong life,"—we are

told this in Scripture. It is very unhealthy to indulge in eating, drinking, ease, or pleasure. Things that are good in themselves, and even necessary, are made bad by indulgence. And this sort of indulgence leads people to think so much more of their bodies than they do of their souls, and so much more of this world than they do of the next, that they are not unlikely to forget their souls and their future state altogether.

Meditate sometimes on Temperance and Sobriety. You will find many opportunities of bringing these virtues into daily use. Suppose you are living in some sort of service where your food is provided. If you are now and then denied some article of food, a little comfort which you like and enjoy, don't vex over it, don't say it is hard to go without it. Remember temperance. If you have enough food to support life healthily, be thankful, and don't grieve at the temporary withdrawal of a comfort. Give up cheerfully, and make a virtue of it. Be the first to set a good example by taking such a little trouble pleasantly. Don't class yourselves among those ignorant women who say they can't do without their beer, or their meat for supper or for breakfast, or their morning's sleep, or their company. We can all of us do without these things, and all other luxuries. And if you cannot give up luxuries cheerfully, you are in bondage to the body; you are binding yourself with a chain which will grow stronger and stronger, till the soul itself suffers like a slave from its weight.

The healthiest people, with the clearest intellect, the soundest judgment, and the strongest will, have been found to lead temperate, sober, and regular lives. They have been drinkers of water, seldom indulging in beer, wine, or spirit; eating sparely of meat, never more than once a day; early risers, and in the habit of going to bed with regularity at a moderately early hour. They have been people not living in hot rooms, nor sleeping in luxuriously soft beds, nor frequenting places of amusement. They have been people who have had plenty to do, and who have done their work with regularity and method, and who have led moral lives, and kept their passions in strict subjection.

So temperance and sobriety have a reward even in this life.

If the money spent in drinking, in foolish extravagances in eating, in company, in unnecessary ornaments in dress, and in many other little intemperate ways and doings, could all be put together, would it not amount to a large sum? Would it not buy good clothes for many a family, build many comfortable houses, pay the rent of many a field, and set up many persons in good trades? And should we not feel that our temperance was rewarded, even in this world, if we could thus surround ourselves with wholesome comforts, and help those we love to begin life well?

We must pray for grace to lead sober and temperate lives. We shall get our reward in this life in health and strength. And we shall, by becoming the conquerors of ourselves, gain that inward strength that helps the soul on its way of self-denial for the love of God, which is the way of salvation and everlasting happiness.

CHAPTER XL

REVERENCE.

You have read, in the chapters that precede this chapter, of modesty, and of temperance, and sobriety. We are now going to consider what Reverence is.

Reverence is a virtue very much forgotten. Scarcely known by many; very seldom thought of by the generality of young girls and women.

That this should be the case is really a misfortune; for reverence is a beautiful thing. It ennobles all who practise it; and those who forget it, or know nothing about it, are very inferior to what they might be, had they ever known reverence, and loved and practised it.

Reverence includes a great deal. It is impossible to imagine a girl of a reverential turn of mind not being also modest, and sober, and temperate too.

It is often remarked that people have a much more dashing way of doing things now than they had in "the old times." This may not always be good; and it is quite sure, that in matters affecting the soul it is bad.

Reverence about holy things, reverence for holy Church, is good. We see many girls who intend, and try, to save their souls, who are not reverential. How is this?

A good girl gets up early, does her morning's work

fast and well, and all that she may go to Mass, and get there in good time. That is right.

But when she gets to the church-door, she is still in the same fast, unceremonious state of mind as she was when she cleaned the grate; and that is a great pity. When she gets to the church-door, she pushes her way; she takes holy water without a thought or a prayer, she walks fast to her place, she elbows away any one who may be there, and then she drops on her knees and begins to say some prayers, and has perhaps said two or three before her hurry of mind is past, and she is sufficiently composed to think of where she is, why she is there, to whom she is speaking, and whether or not she sincerely wishes to be heard. Now it is a pity for a good girl to get into this way. She can so easily cure herself. And the cure is, to try to gain reverence. Reverence is a virtue for a Catholic to esteem very highly, for it belongs peculiarly to the character of a Christian. Thoughts and things worthy of reverence are put before them; it is a pity to see them going the way of the thoughtless world, and never practising reverence, and scarcely knowing what it is.

We are advised in holy books to make, as we enter the church, an act of love to God: to desire to worship His glorious majesty as well as we are able, and with great thankfulness to humiliate ourselves in His sight. If this is done truly, quiet manners and gentle actions will grow naturally out of so sweet and solemn a state of mind.

If you know what reverence is yourself, you will respect it in other people. You will not talk loud, or do any thing to distract any one when they are praying. You will not shut doors loudly, or make any unnecessary noise, in the neighbourhood of any place where people are praying, or reading devout books, or waiting to go to confession. You will never do any thing to disturb that reverence that ought to be reigning in such persons' minds. If you should ever be a servant in a priest's house, or ever have any work to do near a chapel, you will remember this, and be reverential yourself, and careful to preserve reverence in other people.

Wherever you may be in life, or whoever you may know, never allow holy people or holy things to be spoken of irreverently in your hearing. Never let any one, for the sake of pretending to be clever, ridicule any thing that ought to be respected. If you ever hear any one make a joke of a priest, have as little as possible to do with that person. Never allow people to speak too freely of bishops, priests, or nuns. Let no ridicule be thrown upon their looks, or manners, or customs, or dress, or any thing that belongs to them. Reverence demands that great respect should be felt towards those who fill high places in the Church of God. Out of reverence for what God has ordained, let us respect those who do His work in the Church.

Reverence of heart will show itself in outward tokens. When a priest enters our house or our room, we should rise up, welcome him with respect, remembering whose servant he is; and no matter how kind or condescending he may be, we should never forget the great and holy place he fills in the Church of Christ, and to what high privileges those persons are called who have the power of saying Mass, and administering the Sacraments. If we are in authority over any persons, we should see that this reverence is remembered by them as well as by ourselves. And in bringing up children we should carefully inculcate the same feeling. We revere God when we revere His priests.

It is reverential to behave with propriety in any place where Mass is said, even if the Adorable Sacrament is not there. In that great Presence we cannot be too reverential—we cannot be reverential enough; for we are in the presence of God Himself. And acts of love and contrition, faith and hope, are the worship we should pay Him there with all the reverence of which we are capable. And in those places where Mass is sometimes said, in a private chapel, or where missions are only beginning, in a room set apart as a chapel, it is reverent to preserve a composed and thoughtful state of mind. Suppose, for instance, that you are cleaning a chapel, only a private chapel perhaps, where Mass is said occasionally, it would be irreverent to do it noisily, singing merry songs, talking and laughing loudly. It would, on the contrary, be thoughtful and reverent to entertain your soul with thoughts of the great Presence that is there sometimes, of the prayers, perhaps the holy Communions there offered up and enjoyed; of the goodness, and mercy, and majesty of God. With these thoughts, you would do your work with a feeling of devotion, your conscience feelingly alive, your heart making acts of love. This would be working in the service of God; and such reverence would bring comfort and health to your soul.

From reverential motives we should not give a little child a crucifix to make a plaything of; or let it turn a figure of a saint into a doll, or use it as a hammer. You may very easily teach a child the difference between objects intended to excite devotion and mere playthings and tools. It is doing right towards a child to make it understand this. And very early will the pure heart of an innocent child learn reverence, if you will let it.

Such distinctions as these are the result of education, and all pleasing and refined feelings, very agreeable to our neighbours and very wholesome for ourselves. All good Catholic girls are, by the mere fact of their knowing their religion, sufficiently instructed to comprehend and practise reverence. None but the coarse and the rude and the vulgar will despise this beautiful virtue. Beautiful as it is, all can practise it ; and the experience of every heart, after having once been led to think about it, will be a sufficient instructor on the subject.

The Church teaches reverence to us. Don't we all know the reverence which holy Church prescribes towards the sacred vessels? When a chalice has been used for Mass, only a priest's hand may touch it. The same reverence is observed towards the paten ; you may not touch it. Why? The paten and the chalice are to be treated with this reverence because the sacred Body and Blood, under the appearance of bread and wine, have rested in them. The same reverence is observed towards the corporal, which is the name of the linen cloth on which the priest places the Blessed Sacrament; only the priest's hand touches it. When it is to be cleaned, you cannot touch it. It is a priest who must touch it ; and not till he has washed it in water can you take it and go on with its washing, and get it again ready for being used at Mass. Do not these regulations teach us reverence?

In Rome are preserved the stairs down which our Blessed Lord went from the house of Pilate. They are in a building erected for them; and there is a little chapel at the top. They are called the Holy Stairs. Every one who goes up those stairs goes up them on their knees. Our beloved Pope has gone up those stairs upon his knees. Is not this reverence?

From the same motive, when we go to see the Pope, we do not kiss his hand, as is the custom with earthly monarchs. We think of him as the successor of St. Peter, as the head of the Church to which we belong, as one to whom we owe obedience, with whom God Himself works to preserve the Church, and to keep her doctrines perfect. We kneel down reverently and kiss his foot; and to remind us at that moment of Jesus, he wears a cross upon the shoe that covers it. This too is reverence; but it is also more, it is an act of homage and a declaration of faith.

A good person who worships God, and reverences persons, places, and things for God's sake, is sure to be a pleasant person. It is a virtue which finds many opportunities of practice in private life. A servant will treat with that sort of reverence that is called *respect* her employers, the servants placed over her, the guests and relations that come to the house. A child will treat with reverence her parents, her teachers, the friends of her family, and all who have treated her parents or herself with sympathy and kindness. A person who understands what reverence is will joyfully be reverential towards the aged, the sick, the unhappy, the afflicted, and the unfortunate.

She will not be careless of her duties, or thoughtless in a place of trust. She will not give saucy answers or bold looks; as was said in the beginning of this chapter, she will be modest and temperate and sober. You know why she will be all this. Because she will have learnt to reverence that great gift of God; that gift so loved of our Lord, that He died to save it, and lives again to feed and strengthen it, and keeps the fountain of His precious blood for ever running to cleanse it—her own soul. She will reverence her soul for Jesus' sake; she will keep that precious soul, that He has died to save, as pure as she possibly can. And she will walk through life with reverence.

CHAPTER XII.

CARELESSNESS.

CARELESSNESS is the reverse of reverence. A careless person has little thought about any thing. 'I don't care,' 'Never mind,' 'That's nothing to me,' are her commonest expressions;—and all these expressions mean bad and careless states of mind. 'I don't care' means, in her mouth, that she has no thought about what she ought to think about, no interest in duties which ought to interest her. 'Never mind' in her mouth means that she is not going to take any thing to heart, that she is not going to try to do things well, or to make amends for what she has done, or to take any serious thought about the duties and responsibilities that belong to the state of life in which, by the providence of God, she is placed. And 'That's nothing to me' in her mouth means that she has no respect for any person or thing; and that she is never going to cultivate a spirit of reverence, or be any thing but a low-minded slave, who works because she is obliged to work, and who has no notion of rising to the happy and independent state of mind where people are masters of their work, fully understand their duties, and have a joyful feeling of honour when they perform them well, and find themselves valued and respected.

Some careless people have the character of being

very good-tempered.. "A good-tempered, careless girl" is a very common character, and a very bad one. For if that girl knew how little to be respected a careless girl is in the eyes of the wise and good, she would be rather sad than cheerful. And if she is only good-tempered because she does not care, then a poor idiot is as good-tempered as she is; and such good-temper in a reasonable being, who is thoroughly careless and without thought, only shows how little she understands her own badness and her miserable uselessness.

These good-tempered, careless people do all the things that a modest, recollected girl with a reverential mind never does. They stare about at Mass, don't care how they disturb people, or what disedification they give. They are noisy, and disrespectful, and would as soon laugh at a holy thing as not, if any thing droll was said about it. They take no thought or care about any thing. They expect things to go right just the same, whether they do right or wrong. They are always selfish; for selfishness is generally at the bottom of carelessness. Careless girls can take care of their own interests, if they neglect their employer's.

Careless servants destroy the health of children, the tempers of children, and sometimes even injure the morals of children. They destroy their employer's property. They are wasteful of food and coals. They let food go bad because they are too careless to look after it properly. They use things intended for the parlour in the kitchen; break a fine china dish, perhaps belonging to a dinner-set of value, because they are too careless to get the common kitchen plate that ought to be used. They bring bad customs into a house, and attract bad company to it. They are too careless to recollect that friends ought not to be allowed to come at late hours to a house, and that many people ought not to be allowed to come at all. So, in a respectable house, a careless servant may do incalculable mischief. She may injure the children, destroy property, waste money, change good customs, get a good family evil-spoken of, and receive bad company. And all this because she takes no thought about her duties, has no reverence in her heart, and has no better words than, "Oh, never mind, never mind," for every thing.

But she ought to mind. Such women and girls have found themselves cast upon the world because no one would employ them; and have got from one state of misery to another, till they have been found in the lowest condition imaginable; and surely they had learnt to care then. But then, as far as relates to the affairs of this world, it is too late. They can never get back again into good service or places of trust. They must be content to get but a miserable sort of living, perhaps, for the rest of their days.

But if trouble and misery should have made this careless person think of her soul, it will have done a good work for her in the end; for careless people do not take proper care of their souls. And this is the greatest evil of carelessness. You can understand this by the exercise of your own common sense in a moment. Try to make the case your own. Do you think that if you were habitually careless about your work—about cleaning your master's boots in the morning, sometimes doing them, and sometimes not; always requiring to be asked for them, and often getting a well-deserved scolding; if you were careless about lighting your kitchen-fire, using twice as much wood as was necessary; careless about the meat, not trying to keep it good, or not trying to dress the food properly, spoiling some and wasting some, and giving away what wasn't yours, and letting people help themselves, and take things that you ought to have kept for another day,—if you were thus habitually and constantly careless about your work, do you not think that you would be habitually and constantly careless about your soul? "Yes," I can fancy I hear you answer,—"yes, I think I should."

Now try again,—if you fancy yourself careless of what is said to you. Leaving doors open that ought to be locked; letting people placed under you do what you know is forbidden; and if you fancy yourself perpetually doing what your employer has told you not to do, all from carelessness, and because you don't try to mend your ways or to remember your orders,—don't you think that you will also forget from carelessness the commands of God, and the instructions of the priest? Yes; people who are careless about their common duties in this world, are careless also of those great duties by which we are intended to get to everlasting happiness in the nextworld. Careless people by their every-day actions keep their souls in danger, and get out of that good habit of recollection that is of so much benefit to them. Some people seem to be stupidly careless. I suppose these persons have not had opportunities of learning any thing, and may not, perhaps, naturally be very clever. But these careless, stupid girls can improve. Trying to think, trying to give their whole attention to the work in hand, determining to remember, doing their best to understand, and praying to their patron saint, and encouraging themselves with the happy thought that God sees, and helps, and loves them,—these are the best things to do in order to improve; and the girl who tries in this way with courage and perseverance is sure to succeed; for if she is naturally rather stupid, carelessness may be as much a misfortune as a fault. She may not take care, or think with steadiness, because she is ignorant and has grown up in careless ways for want of a teacher, and has never been put in the way of teaching herself.

I will tell you what happened to one of those careless, stupid girls.

Her aunt was a housemaid in a family where two were kept; and she got her mistress's leave to have her niece, who was called Celia Smith, as the servant under her. Celia was stupid and careless. Her aunt talked, and tried to show her how to do things; and Celia gaped and stared and said, "Oh, yes; she knew,—oh, yes, that would do; oh, never mind." Her aunt would then watch her as she did her work, and Celia would do every thing wrong. She could never do things at the right time, or put things in their proper places, or keep things to their proper uses.

The baths were not filled; bellows, brushes, black-lead, and twenty other things, were lost and found every day. She dusted the rooms with the chamber-towels, and used the dusters for floor-cloths. Then she was always dirty; her face had black-lead on it; her apron would be streaming wet; her hair was always pulled into dreadful disorder, and nearly every day she stepped on her gown and tore it.

Celia's aunt was an excellent woman, and a very good servant. Every thing she did, she did well—active, clever, diligent, and full of recollectedness and reverence; she was kind, and generous-hearted, and honest, and honourable. At last this good woman thought that Celia ought not to be kept. Every thing she did had to be done twice over, and she wore things out improperly, and dirtied the furniture; and so her honourable-minded aunt thought that she ought to send Celia away. She had talked to her very often, prayed for her, cried over her,—all was of no use. Celia was not to be corrected; she was a poor, stupid, careless girl, and she was to go home disgraced. Then something happened; and Celia was cured at once. You see even the stupid can improve, and the most careless may mend; for Celia was cured. Something happened, and she never was careless again. This was what happened. Frightful screams were heard from the morning sitting-room one day, and the master of the house first rushed in. There stood Celia one dreadful mass of flames. Her master could scarcely see who it was, so quickly the flames flashed up, and so dreadful did she look; for all her thick hair was in flames and smoke. The gentleman threw her down, and with the hearth-rug and the table-cover and his own great-coat stifled the flames. She was carried up-stairs, and as her burnt clothes dropped off, lumps of flesh, all charred black, dropped off too. It was dreadful. Every one said she could not live. The agony she suffered no words can describe. She never spoke: no one asked her to speak. Her aunt held a crucifix before her, but no one could decide if she saw or not. Eyelashes and eyebrows were burnt off, and the eyelids so injured that she could not close them.

The kind good Christians with whom she lived spared no trouble nor expense; and, notwithstanding her dreadful burns, Celia lived. It was three months before she could move; and then she was supported by a person on each side. Time went on, and no one asked Celia how the accident had happened: the doctor had said that she was not to be agitated; and the least thing would so upset her poor injured nerves, that even a kind smile would make her cry for hours. So she was treated like a thing only half alive, and nursed tenderly for three months more. Then one day she said to her aunt, "Aunt, do you know what set me in flames?"

The aunt, surprised at such a question, said, "Oh, yes, my dear, the fire in the morning room."

"What set me in flames was carelessness; yes, carelessness," said Celia solemnly. "I have never felt well enough to tell till to-day,—I think carelessness is almost a sin; see what it leads to—carelessness set me in flames, put the whole house and all the lives in it in danger, and nearly brought me to the grave in my stupid careless state; for I couldn't care about any thing. I had as little care about my soul as about my worldly duties, and I was as dull about my salvation as I was about my work."

"Well, Celia," said her aunt, "then we may thank God if that is over now. One day you shall tell me how it was you caught fire."

"I will tell you now," said Celia. "You had sent me to make up the fire, sweep the hearth, and whiten the hearth-stone."

"Yes," said her aunt, "I remember."

"I cleaned the hearth; I had let the white stone get on the black grate. I therefore went for some black-lead, and the brushes to clean it off,—I had tried to take it off with the soap and water that I had for the hearth-stone, and I had made a large ugly place of it."

"Well," said her aunt, smiling kindly, "and what did my careless niece do next?"

"Yes, you had a careless niece indeed," said Celia. "The next thing she did was to black-lead the spot on the grate; then, to help herself up from the rug on which she was kneeling."

"You ought to have turned back the rug," said her aunt quickly.

"Yes, I knew that," said Celia; "but *never mind* was in my heart then. I did not turn back the rug. In getting up, I helped myself to rise by putting my fingers on the marble chimney-piece. So, when I stood up, I saw the marks of my black fingers on the white slab."

"Oh dear, oh dear," sighed her aunt. "But you do not tell me how you caught fire."

"I am coming to that," said Celia, with a faint smile, and a weak voice; for she was getting tired of even this little amount of exertion. "I told you it was carelessness; I will prove it now. When I saw the finger-marks, I got some clean soap and water to take them out; and I took them out."

"The work was finished, then, I suppose," said her aunt.

"No; for in washing the white marble slab, I had let the soap and water make small splashes all over the lower part of the looking-glass that is over the chimney-piece. I could not reach to the highest splashes as I stood; so I got a stool and stood on that, and leant forward on the chimney-piece, and my gown must have touched the fire, for the flames burst up, and scorched my face before I could scream for help. I jumped off the stool, master rushed in, and all the rest you know. Aunt, dear aunt, I shall never be careless again."

Celia Smith spoke truly; she never was careless again. She became a thoughtful, steady, trustworthy servant; and when her aunt married, three years after, she took the place of upper housemaid herself. As she learnt to think of her work and her duties, she thought also of her soul, and soon led that life that every Catholic woman ought to lead, serving God in her daily tasks and duties, doing every thing to His honour, and adorning the place she filled in the Church of Christ with her many good works.

You may know from this story that the most stupid and careless girls may become wise and thoughtful. Prayer and painstaking may do for you what this terrible accident and illness did for Celia Smith. All her life she will wear the marks of her carelessness. She will always be a little lame from the shrinking of the sinews of one leg. She will always be seamed and scarred. But she will always be loved, respected, and valued. She is the trusty friend of her master and mistress; a good example to all around her; and she is saving her soul in the state of life in which her Heavenly Father placed her; never careless about any thing—neither about her body or her soul—neither about this world or the next; but by practising Christian virtues she makes herself valued and loved.

In the case of Celia Smith, she only seriously hurt herself. She injured her master's property by her carelessness; but her good aunt took care that this injury should not be to any great amount, so she only seriously hurt herself. But a very melancholy part of the conduct of careless people is, that they generally injure other people more than themselves. Only very lately, a large number of persons were poisoned, and many died, in consequence of a careless tradesman leaving arsenic open in such a careless manner, that it was sold for another thing, and put into sweetmeats, to the dreadful injury of a large number of persons. Dirty, careless cooks have poisoned whole families, and killed many, by not cleaning their copper pans carefully. A careless servant, not long ago, set fire to a sofa by placing a candle near it. This person went out of the room without perceiving what had happened. Soon the whole room was in a blaze. No lives, happily, were lost; but the damage done to valuable property was very large, and of a sort never to be remedied. A woman in a large town, smelt a strong smell of gas in the shop at the front of the house. She knew by the smell that the gas was escaping; she also knew that gas will take fire. Yet she walked into the shop with a lighted candle in her hand. The whole of the air in the shop being mingled with gas, it took fire, and an explosion occurred. It knocked the shop-front out, and killed two people sleeping in a room above. The woman herself was only knocked backward, and escaped with bruises. How would any good Catholic girl, a servant at a shop, feel if she had done this?

If you are careless, pray for strength, and cure yourself; you can if you try.

CHAPTER XIII.

GOOD MANAGEMENT.

To be a good manager is to be a very good thing; it is to be a friend to others and a friend to yourself.

There are several cases in which good management is very desirable. We will think of a few.

We will think of the management of persons, of the management of property, of the management of work, and of the management of time.

Almost every one, at some period of their lives, have to do with children. It is very necessary to know how to manage them. As to their health, you will be under orders on that subject, if you take care of other people's children; the mother or the upper-nurse will take that responsibility off your hands. But the management of the children's tempers and dispositions may belong to you as much as to others; in their walks, in their play, and at all times when you and they are together, you must be careful of the management of their tempers and dispositions.

You must never let a child feel you are angry; you must be gentle and very patient with all children. Never mind how trying they may be; there is something solemn and holy in a child's innocence, and in the thought of our Blessed Lord having clothed His glorious majesty in the weak flesh of an infant. The recollection, too, of how much nearer that child is to heaven than you are should tame and subdue any feelings of vexation and anger that may rise in your heart. If that child were to die in your arms, he would be instantly a glorious saint,—instantly able to stand in the presence of God,— instantly able to praise and magnify our Blessed Lord and Redeemer in a manner more perfect than may ever be ours, and instantly able to pray for you as you cannot pray for yourself. This thought ought always to be joined to the care of a child. It will be part of your duty to see, as far as is in your power, that that child shall keep its goodness and purity, and that its natural passions shall not be roused; for every time the passions are roused in a child they increase in strength and vigour, and they will do so until the child can himself battle with his passions and conquer them. Never, then, rouse a child's passions, or let any other person rouse them. People tease children for amusement sometimes. It is really wrong to do this: it is trying to bring out the evil of a child's nature instead of the good.

Never reproach a child. If a child has done wrong, so as to require correction, the proper person should correct it; but no one should reproach it. All such expressions as, "Now, don't be naughty, as you were yesterday," and all such reproachful words as, "O you wicked child!" should be avoided. A child may require to be ruled; but one who understands the management of children will never be reproachful about the past, or call a child wicked, or do any thing to keep alive the remembrance of past naughtiness. This kind of keeping up of grievances only teases a child, and makes it remember that it can be naughty, and puts it in mind of being naughty again.

Very seldom threaten a child; and if a child is threatened, never threaten it with a punishment that you have no right to give; never say, for instance, that you will send a child to bed without its supper, when you know that the child for its health's sake must have its supper, and that you have no right to enforce such a punishment. A clever child will know this; and if it holds out obstinately in its fault, you will be obliged to yield, and the child has conquered. This sort of foolish contest is very bad management, and has injured many dispositions.

Never have contests of words with a child. "I didn't," "You did," "I did," "You didn't," is all very bad, and should not be allowed. Children often like a dispute. A good manager won't dispute. If she sees this sort of temper coming on a child, she will draw off its attention quickly to something else. Showing a picture, telling a story, or a playful run across the room, is a better stop to a dispute than any orders of "Hold your tongue! you are not to speak again, miss;" which the child can disobey if it likes. A good manager will do this.

This advice is good for all girls who have the charge of younger girls in schools, as happens sometimes. In working-classes, sometimes the elder girls teach the younger. The elder girls have power in some things, and they should learn how to manage it with propriety; that is, for the good of those they teach, and for the benefit of their own souls. All power is a trust; all who have power should manage it as they would any other trust, for good, and not for evil. If you have to teach a child or any older person, never teach with pride or scorn, or in a hurrying or ordering sort of way, as if the task was disagreeable to you, and you chose to do it with ill-temper, rudeness, or contempt. The person you teach may be stupid. You must manage to instruct her without showing her that you think her stupid. To get that character would discourage many timid girls, and be disagreeable to any child. Take pains with her. Remember that you yourself may be stupid, as far as the gift of teaching is concerned. Manage to find out how the girl you teach can easiest receive knowledge, and then try to give it to her in the way pleasantest to her, even if it should be in the way least pleasant to you. You will soon get power over that girl's mind and attention, if you are a good teacher; and then you can, after she has got knowledge enough to understand, bring her to your own ways.

It is right to use a little gentle, kind management, so as to avoid vexing and irritating or discouraging the young. Remember this in any place of authority that you may be called upon to fill.

The management of sick people is a thing to be studied with great attention by all who have to do with the sick. A good, cheerful, forbearing, attentive nurse, who never makes a trouble of her duties, is a great help to the doctor, as well as a great comfort to the invalid.

And it may happen that some of you may have the trial of a dear friend living in sin. You may see and know that your relative or near friend is so living, and to you may fall the difficult task of managing a sinner. This will require great tenderness and great humility on your part, or you will certainly fail to manage well. The end of all you do or say must be to bring that sinner to repentance and amendment. It is an end seldom attained by talking: patience, loving entreaties offered when the person's mind is in a fit state to accept them, constant good example, and many prayers,—these are the things that God blesses, and you must practise them. If a time comes when the wrong-doer seems to be doing better, manage to let it be seen that you are thankful and glad, but don't make loud observations about it. The first steps of a returning sinner are always timid; it will require loving management not to frighten back that precious soul.

The management of property often comes to the lot of women. Every body has something of her own to take care of, or she has something of value belonging to other people intrusted to her care and management. In both cases it is a duty to learn the best way of managing what you have; and having got this knowledge, it is a duty to practise it.

The wilful waste that people practise in this world is something sad to think about. If you see a poor, thin, slatternly woman, with a torn cap, disordered hair, greasy gown, trolloping skirt, dirty ragged stockings, thin slippers, or shoes down at the heels and with holes at the sides,—if you see such a woman or girl standing about, staring up and down the street, or running constantly out of the house to gaze at passers-by and exchange idle words with them, you may be sure that such a person has never learnt how to manage well; *has never tried to learn*, which is a great disgrace; and is a tiresome daughter, an unsatisfactory servant, or a wasteful wife and a bad mother. And yet hundreds of Catholics are just such women as you read of here. It is a sorrowful thing. Make up your minds now as you read that you will never be such a woman as that.

There are great complaints about drunken men very often; how they spend their time and money at public-houses, and neglect their families and homes. Depend upon it, if they had well-managed homes and well-managed families, they would not so often be absent from those homes; and they would not so often seek bad company if they found good company at their own fireside.

A bad manager not only ruins the children who are about her by not knowing how to manage either their minds or their bodies, but she keeps her house so poor, that poverty often pinches when its presence ought scarcely to be felt. You ought all to consider this; for many young girls have to keep their fathers' houses, and have the care of the younger children given up to them. Perhaps the mother is dead; perhaps she is in the hospital; perhaps she is so sick at home that she cannot do the work that belongs to the mother and the mistress of the house. Then the elder girl has to do a woman's work, and take a woman's thought about things; and much misery may arise from her never having thought of what good management means. There was a girl once—she is still alive, and a woman now—who was called very early to do a good manager's work in her father's house. Her father was a fisherman, and they lived in a little fishing-village by the sea-side, far away from any large town. The man had a share with other men in some fishing-boats, and he had crab-pots and lobster-pots of his own. These crab-pots and lobster-pots are baskets, made something like wire mouse-traps, only very much larger. They are baited with food such as these shell-fish like, and sunk in the sea in places frequented by the fish. The crabs and lobsters enter by a hole, which is a passage narrower at the end than at the entrance, and when once in they can't get out.

The fisherman was called James Webster. He was seldom at home, and was often out all night. His wife had a busy life. She prepared the food for the lobster-pots, and made her husband a dinner of vegetables or meat, baked in a strong crust, to carry away with him, wrapped in a clean cloth, when he left home. She had a great deal of sewing to do for her husband; for he required strong clothes, and decent clothes too, when he went with his cart and pony to the houses of the gentry to sell his fish, which he was often obliged to do if he had not a ready sale in any other way. She had the garden to take care of; for they could not afford to pay for labour, and they wanted winter-potatoes, and plenty of carrots both for the pony and themselves. Then there were five children to take care of, and three to send to school. And fish had to be salted, and salmon had to be dried in the right season, and whiting and cod at other times; for they sold dried fish in the winter, and they could not sell it unless it was well done. The washing, the making and mending of clothes, and the baking, were all done at home. Mary Webster worked very hard and very well; for she was an excellent manager. And though her husband's trade was an uncertain one,—in which in the plentiful fish-seasons he sometimes made two and three pounds a week, and then for days and weeks in winter never made a single penny, —yet Mary had always the money stored up from the good times to provide with in the bad times; and not one of that family wanted food or clothing or firing. James had a comfortable clean fireside to come to at all times, with something to eat in the cupboard, and a good bed to lie down on to rest in thankfulness.

There were two women in the village, who were the wives of the men who were partners with James Webster in the property of the fishing-boats. The three men had equal shares in the boats; they worked together, and divided equally the fish that were caught. But these women had not homes like Mary Webster's. Their advantages in life appeared to be in every respect equal. But they were half starved in the winter; never tidy winter or summer; never clean as the Websters; and not taught like them, for they had no money to spend on sending their children to school. They agreed in saying that Mary Webster was the most wonderful woman in the parish; and they said that they did not know how she did it.

Suddenly a fever ran through the village. The wives of Webster's partners both took it. Mary helped to nurse them. Coming home one night from a day's nursing, she fell over a broom that an untidy child had left on the ground; the handle rolled from under her foot, and in falling she sprained her back. It was a very severe strain; she was confined to her bed, and the loss of her labour and care was a sad thing for her family; and she had to take the eldest girl, Jane, from school, to be the mistress of the house.

Of course Jane acted under her mother's instructions; and I can assure you, that at twelve years old she managed every thing, except the washing, for which they had to hire now and then. It seemed more strange because Jane was very small. She used to stand on a stool to make bread; but she made it, and very good it was. Her mother grew weak in consequence of being confined to her bed; and when her back got better, she fell into a consumption, and in two years she died. At fourteen, Jane had the whole management of that house and family fall on her.

Her father used to say, "She is only fourteen, but she could not do better, or behave more steadily, or manage the young ones and the property with more thought, if she were forty. May God bless my good, steady, managing child!"

Having read this instance of good management, in the case of a child fourteen years of age, you must never make your youth an excuse for want of knowledge, care, and steadiness. You can be steady, thoughtful, and managing, at a very early age, if you determine to be so by God's grace, and diligently try to succeed.

It is good to know how to manage your own property; but it becomes doubly a duty to manage well, when the property of other persons is given to your care. The sight of waste is shocking, or ought to be shocking, to a Christian. When a Christian woman undertakes the charge of property which is not her own, she ought honourably to fulfil her trust, and be scrupulously careful in her management of things committed to her care.

You will understand this better by thinking for a minute how easy it is to waste things. Waste in a servant is robbery of her master. She is paid to take care of things, and to fill her place properly. She wastes what she has the care of, and her master has to pay for all she has wasted; and by wasting it, she has deprived him of the money, and of the things that money bought. This is unworthy of a Christian. Consider the case of a general servant in a tradesman's family, where all necessary things are amply provided, and many pleasant luxuries and comforts allowed. That woman receives good wages, and she has a variety of things in her charge.

Now it is very easy to waste a little milk every day. I have seen a girl, when she wanted the jug, throw at least a pennyworth of milk out on the stones of the yard, and say, "Oh, I wanted the jug for hot water." A pennyworth wasted every day will be about thirty shillings a year.

It is very easy to waste coals; keeping a roaring fire when there is no cooking to do is a very common way. I heard a girl say, "I always make the fire roar of an evening; it is so pleasant to listen to when I am sitting still." Such a girl would waste easily a ton of coals every quarter; which would be about five pounds a year.

It is very easy to waste food. Bread, meat, and

vegetables, are easily wasted,—by being ill taken care of, by being badly cooked, by being dirtily put away, by being forgotten when cold; by dressing fresh meat before the cooked meat is finished; by being improperly given away. I knew a girl who was ordered to give the driver of a cart his dinner, as he had done some work for her master. So she placed before him the most expensive thing in the house; a piece of meat which had been salted in a particular way, and was worth two shillings a pound. So the carter made a great dinner off it; it had been intended for the parlour breakfast-table, and it was never fit to appear there again. The man would have been quite as well pleased with a couple of mutton-chops; but the silly girl had given him a dinner worth three shillings. In these ways, three shillings a week may easily be wasted; that is seven pounds sixteen shillings a year. You can calculate that, in these instances only, a woman may waste more than fourteen pounds a year. And so her carelessness and want of management has taken fourteen pounds out of her master's purse; this is very like robbery, is it not?

There are some persons, who have not had the blessing of being as well taught as the girls are for whom this book is written, who say that they are not required to do their best. They say that if they do not wilfully, with a fixed intention, waste their employer's goods, they are not to blame for "*letting things go,*" as the expression is; for being, that is, profuse, and extravagant, and bad managers. If they do not steal, they think it is all well. They say there is no necessity laid upon them to take care, and to save. If they are not really dishonest, and do not actually sell their master's goods, and take money for themselves out of the sale, they say that they do no harm by giving away to their friends, and letting their friends make presents to them in return. In fact, they undertake the duties of a situation; they agree to receive food, and wages, and the accommodations of a house, for the performance of those duties; and then they enter upon them with the fixed intention of *not* doing their best. I entreat you, my dear friends, never to belong to this most mean class of persons. We have no example given us for imitation that can teach us this. Think of our Blessed Lady, of St. Joseph, of your own patron Saint. Did they learn such evil lessons? did they yield to such temptations? did they earn their glorious places in Heaven by *not* doing their best? There is often great piety in striving to do your best. But to do your best in the management of another person's property is scarcely more than common honesty in the eyes of a good Catholic. If you once begin upon this plan of not trying to do your best, you will be led farther than you expect. You will find yourself tempted by the devil to carry the same idea into effect in the concerns of your soul. It is a very dangerous course, as well as a mean and dishonourable one. It is a course which you must never allow yourselves even to think of pursuing. There is a good old saying, "Wilful waste makes woful want." It is a very true one. If employers have a proper knowledge of how their property ought to be managed, they would be very foolish to keep a wasteful servant about them. Wasteful servants get out of place again and again;

and sad, and full of want, is often their friendless end.

The management of work is a very important thing to a Catholic. Very often most serious things depend upon this. There are many places, both in towns and in the country, where very clever management of work is required to enable the servant to get to Mass on days of obligation, and to get with comfort to her duties. Thought, experience, courage, industry, and perseverance, all practised with frequent prayer, will enable a servant to manage these difficulties without any doubt. If she does her part with a true, honest, and faithful heart, God will help her. Don't give in to the thought that your work is to be neglected for your duties. This can very seldom be necessary; and you ought not to yield to the idea. A hard struggle it may be to manage your work; but try to conquer, and don't neglect a single thing, if you can by any management avoid it. This double faithfulness, both to the life of your soul, and that life of labour which God has ordained for your body, will get you great rewards from our Blessed Lord. Your state in life, even if it is one of very hard work, is that dear Lord's choosing for you. You may then do the work belonging to it for His sake. Managing your work, then, is doing God's will, and you may consider it as a part of the service you owe to Him; for it is the fulfilling of His adorable will. Thus, by good management, to "*make time*," as people say, for Mass and Confession, becomes something more than a duty performed; it becomes a merit gained. However hard you work, you are very happy if you can manage to accomplish it in this Christian way; for you will find many a reward ready for you in the presence of God when you die, won by good management in the state of life which He appointed as your trial. And now we come to the management of Time.

Perhaps you may think that the management of time and the management of work are the same things. No, not quite the same things to a Catholic; for time and *thought* may be considered together now. If you have learnt how to do your work well, you know how to manage time and work. But there is another profit to be taken out of time by a good manager. She can make a treasure of good thoughts of it; and so improve, by the help of the grace of God, very speedily and very certainly in the Christian life.

A girl with her time full of work will therefore do well, not only to keep all grumbling and discontent far away from her, but also to keep these recollections constantly alive,—that it is God's will that she should work, and that she will therefore work well and willingly. She who lives in this state of mind, manages her time well. A hard-worked girl cannot pray on her knees long or often, —cannot give a little of her day to pious reading, and perhaps can only say her Rosary sometimes. This *may be*; but don't allow that it *must be*, without very good cause. However, we will now suppose that it must be. What then? She must manage to make time by saying her prayers at her work. There was a good Irish girl who used to say, "Oh, I have plenty of time for saying my prayers on my knees. I scrub the scullery, the back hall, and the long slate passage, every day. And to keep the servants' rooms clean in this great house, I have to scrub four every week; and I scrub half the day on all Saturdays, besides being on my knees when I black the stoves and light the fires." Surely this very hard-worked girl had learned something of the secret of managing time. Time is the most precious thing we have. And although we have often such a multitude of worldly things to do in it, it yet belongs especially to the soul. For time is given to us for the working out of our souls' salvation; and every thing we do should tend towards that great end. The hardest-worked girl in the world can manage to pray very often. She can easily get a habit of saying prayers for the dead at particular times, or when doing particular things. It need not make her do work badly. We have already said, that as work is ordered by God, we are not to neglect it,—we are always, with great diligence, to do our best. She ought to think often of her next confession, and reckon up the things she is sorry for in her mind, and make strong resolutions against all sin. She ought to think of death, and judgment, and eternity. When she goes to her bed at night, and closes her eyes to rest, she should give herself up to her guardian angel's care. She should never eat without making a real act of thanksgiving, and remembering the sign of the Cross; and many girls at these times make a short prayer for the faithful departed, which is an excellent habit. And it is a pious habit, and one easily learnt, to think, whenever you hear the clock strike, of the rapid flight of time, and to pray that you may never omit your endeavours to manage it well.

These instructions are gathered from holy books, and the practices of pious people. My dear girls, let us all try to learn the value of time, and all pray for grace to manage it well.

CHAPTER XIV.

JUSTICE.

A HOLY writer has told us of justice, that it is a virtue that inclines us to give to every one his own; and first in His great rights in us is God Himself. *Render to Cæsar the things that are Cæsar's, and to God the things that are God's.*

And Justice requires you to keep always in your mind two principles laid down in holy Scripture: "*See thou never do to another what thou wouldst hate to have done to thee by another;*" and "*All things, therefore, whatsoever you would that men should do to you, do you also to them.*"

Justice towards your neighbour, you may observe, is a very easy thing to understand. We have the knowledge of it, as it were naturally, in our own hearts; for we all know what we like and what we dislike; and by that knowledge we are to guide ourselves in our conduct to other people.

Giving to God the things that are God's, is saying in other words that you are not to lose your soul. That God has made you for His service on earth, and to be eternally happy with Him in heaven, and that you owe it to your God and Saviour to save your soul as an act of justice towards Him. And as you go on through life, you will take care of your soul in the way God has appointed. You will keep your conscience awake; try daily to excite your heart to love God more and more. You will thankfully, and with sorrow, and great reverence, take your sins to confession. And you will go to holy Communion with all the love and humility, gratitude and adoration, that your soul can feel.

Thus, being good and persevering members of Christ's Church, you will try on all occasions to do justice to your neighbour.

You will obey the laws of the place in which you live; you will always try to be a peace-maker; and you will act for other people's good before considering your own; you will never be selfish. You will never crave for favours from people; you will not ask for things you have no right to, or require to have more than you ought to want provided for you. You will not judge your own merits too highly. You will not ask more for your services than they deserve, or offer yourself to fill any place for which you are not competent. You will never hurt any one either by word or deed; you will judge every one kindly, and try to think the best of them; and you will do all the good to your neighbour that lies within your power.

These are the duties that belong to justice. Think of them in a practical manner. You are to obey the laws of the place in which you live. You will probably all of you be getting your living in some way or other. You will find laws, or rules, as such laws are often called, in every situation in which you may engage yourself. Justice requires that, if you keep the place, you should obey the laws. No deceit, no little disobediences that may never be found out; justice forbids such things. And if your rulers never find you out, He who is the Ruler of rulers, and who loves justice, will see that you have not remembered His holy law.

You must be a peace-maker. Never, then, begin a quarrel; rather suffer something yourself than quarrel over it. Never foment a quarrel ; never run the risk of making people quarrel by repeating irritating things that they may have said of each other. It is often good amusement, as thoughtless, ignorant girls think, to repeat the annoying things that may have been said to the person of whom they were said. But if you find pleasure in this, condemn yourself for it ; for you have offended against justice.

You will act for other people's good. Selfishness is a very common fault; indeed, it is so deceiving a fault that selfish people scarcely suspect themselves of the failing that others see so plainly. Often, therefore, examine your conscience on this subject, and accuse yourself of this fault, if you think that you are being led away by it. It is a disedifying fault, and one quite contrary to the character of a good Christian, whose example is our Lord Jesus.

You will never crave for favours or distinction; in common language, you will not be greedy after gifts or dignities, or ever think you will offer for a place because you should like the wages or the honour, when you are not really qualified to fulfil its duties.

This last is a fault often committed. A girl thinks she "*should like that place*," and so she offers for it. She ought first to think if she is qualified for that place; if she could do her employer justice in it. It is not her *likings*, but her *fitness*, that she would consider if she was just. You must remember this; for many great wrongs have been committed by girls undertaking work, and responsibilities that they knew nothing about, and were utterly incapable of performing.

You will never ask for things you have no right to, or require to have more provided for you than you ought to want. These faults are often committed. A girl takes a place; she does not like it. What does she do? She does not offer to go. But she asks for this thing and that thing, and for one change and another change; and if she is refused, she says it is hard, and a bad place, and that the people are unkind. Now that is not just. If she knew what the duties of her place would be before she took it, she ought, having agreed to do them, to do her best without complaining, and injuring the character of the persons she serves, and of the situation she offered to fill. And some girls, who live with kind people, find out that by asking for things they can have them. So they ask for gifts, and for days to go out, and for little privileges that their fellow servants have never enjoyed; and all that is contrary to justice. Justice never craves, is never selfish, and never takes advantage of any body. Just people do to others what they would be glad for others to do to them, if their situations were reversed; and they will seek other people's good before their own; and they never rate their own merits too highly, but would feel shame rather than pleasure at taking more favours than were offered to others.

There are other thoughts about justice for persons possessed of any authority. You will probably at some time of your lives have authority reposed in you; and if so, you must remember justice. You must never be unjust in kindness or in rewards. You must never have favourites; you must not treat one person always better than another. You must not believe one person more than another in hearing the two sides of a story, until you have evidence to satisfy you as to which is right. You must not always lay hard burdens on one person by always trying to lighten the burdens on another. You must make arrangements for every one's comfort and health, not taking great care of one person, and scarcely any care at all of another. You must pay people the wages they have earned, and give true characters when characters are asked of you. And when you have to blame or to punish, you must not blame any one more than is deserved, or ever give a heavy punishment for a light offence. You must often think of that great day when the Judge of all men shall judge you; and pray to God to enable you to guide your actions through the whole of your life in such a way as to receive the crown of glory, which only the just shall gain. You will never, my dear reader, if you are just, and in a place of authority, give any presents out of your employer's property, or take little perquisites for yourself which have not been plainly given you. Your authority is given you to guide the house, not to make private gains. All such gains are a mean sort of stealing. You are injuring your soul for the sake of benefiting your body if you make unjust gains, and you are setting a bad example, and hardening the consciences of those who see your guilt and keep silence. Should circumstances seem to oblige you to take more authority on yourself than is usually required in your situation, take the first opportunity of telling your employer *how* you acted, and *why* you acted as you did. Never pretend to those beneath you that you have more power than you really have. Give a good example of truth and justice, and you will find yourself rewarded by our just God and merciful Saviour, by whose grace you have lived a good life in His holy Church.

Of the instructions given in the last few days, the three girls all liked "*Reverence*" very much.

"It was like old thoughts put in a new way," said Anne Wilton. "I am very glad to have had Reverence spoken of."

"I liked '*Justice*,'" said Mary Hardy. "Oh, if I could be just!—I will try."

"Now," said Jane, "I fancy I shall one day be a very good manager. I should like to understand all household affairs, and do them well. And I can't bear carelessness."

In this way they talked, as good girls often talk. In this way they looked forward to the future that they were to spend, getting their own livings in honourable domestic service. Often afterwards they checked themselves when they were on the point of sinning against reverence, or of doing some act of carelessness, or forgetting justice, or good management. And thus, by putting their instructions into practice, they became examples of the virtues they loved.

CHAPTER XV.

OBSERVATION.

ONE thing is very certain, my dear young friends; and it concerns all those who have read this book, or heard it read. It will not have done you any good, or helped you on in the Christian's active life in the smallest degree, if you have heard it, or read it, without using the faculty of Observation.

Girls who have heard and read with observation, understand and remember. And if they understand and remember what has been said, then they have acquired knowledge; and as they go through life, they will use this knowledge to their own and to other people's advantage. These girls are improved by reading.

But girls without observation, though they may have been pleased with some little story for a moment, will not observe. They will not improve; their reading will do them no good.

A curious, impertinent observation in matters which need not concern us is very disagreeable and annoying to both equals and superiors. But, on the other hand, it is very tiresome to have to deal with persons who do not make such intelligent observations as we naturally expect from all who have been properly brought up.

A young servant once went to live with a lady and

gentleman as house-maid and parlour-maid. It was a pretty house, and she liked the work of looking after the many nice things that were placed in her charge very much. When she laid the breakfast, she admired the look of every thing, and particularly she liked a carved chair with rose-coloured velvet seat and back; and she always placed this chair before the urn and tea-things for her mistress, when she made breakfast. When she had done this for about three weeks, her mistress called her into the dining-room, and said with a pleasant smile :

"Mary, you always prepare this room yourself in the morning?"

"Oh, yes, ma'am."

"And you put the room straight after breakfast?"

"Yes, ma'am, always."

"Now, Mary, think of the room as you always find it when we have finished breakfast; think of the chairs you put back in their places. Now what chair do I use at breakfast-time?"

Mary had been thinking as her mistress had desired, so she answered immediately, "You use the light high chair with the cane back and seat." And here Mary grew very rosy.

"Well, Mary, what am I going to say now?"

The lady smiled ; Mary smiled too, and said:

"That I ought to have observed it, and ought not to have put the oak-chair every day."

"Yes; and did you never observe it?"

"I must have observed it, I suppose, because I recollected it just now. But I never observed it properly."

"Well, then, observe properly in future; for a servant without observation neither does justice to herself nor her employer. Now," continued the lady, "I know why you put the oak-chair there for me. It looks so pretty with the rose-colour against the white table-cloth, and the brown-oak, and the shining silver; it makes quite a picture. But can you tell me why I put it aside and take another?"

No; Mary could not guess that.

"Not after observing the shape of the chair?"

No; she could not tell.

"The arms are so high that I knock my elbow when I lift my hand to the tea-urn."

"Oh, yes," said Mary; "and I feel so stupid," she added.

"Help me to fold up those newspapers on the table," said her mistress, "and I will tell you an Arabian tale."

This was the story.

"A merchant was once driving a camel loaded with such things as he sold, and he tied the camel, as he thought securely, to the door of a house into which he went for refreshment. When he came out, the camel was gone. It had got loose and strayed away. So, in great distress, he ran down the road to see after it. He could not see it. The road was crossed by other roads; he could not tell which way the creature had taken; but he turned down one, and still ran on. At last he saw a grave-looking old man, with white hair and a very venerable aspect; and he ran on to him gladly, to ask if he had seen the camel that had strayed. 'Is he lame?' asked the aged man. 'Oh, yes,' said the driver. 'And loaded?' 'Yes.' 'Loaded with grain on the right side, and honey on the left?' 'Oh, yes, venerable father,' exclaimed the driver; 'that is my camel!' 'And lame on the right fore-leg?' said the old man. 'Yes,' exclaimed the other. 'And blind in the left eye?' 'Yes, oh, yes.' 'And with a tooth gone in front?' 'Yes; he has lost a tooth. You have seen my camel; tell me which way he is gone.' 'Oh,' said the aged traveller gravely, 'oh, that, then, was your camel? You may go on, my friend; I have not seen it.' 'You have heard about him, then?' said the camel-driver. 'No,' replied the old man, 'I have neither heard nor seen. I have not spoken with any one but yourself for the day.' The driver grew angry, and seizing the old man roughly, accused him of falsehood, and even of stealing the camel. But the old man answered: 'I have only *observed*, as you might have done. I saw the marks of a camel's foot in the sand; I knew from its wandering steps that it had no driver. I found, from the right foot-mark being always imperfect, that it was lame; I knew from its eating the grass on one side only, that it was blind of one eye; where it had stopped to eat, honey-drops were on one side and grain on the other; and from the tuft of grass that always was left where its teeth had cropped the herbage, I knew that one tooth must be gone. You can follow down this lane, for in this I have observed these things. The camel must be on before you.'"

Mary left the room after hearing this story, to do her work in the bed-rooms. As she entered her master's dressing-room, a thought occurred to her which she had often expressed to one of her fellow-servants,—it was one of Mary's *observations*.

"I wonder why, in the world, it is that master's towels are always wet; wet or damp they always are, every one of them. If I give him dry ones now, they will be too damp to dry a hand on comfortably by the time we go to bed."

With this observation she entered the room and began her work. Two wet towels were hung so as to drip into the bath that her master used daily. Mary wrung these as dry as she could into the bath before she changed the water; then she spread these towels on the frame to dry. She then arranged other towels. When she was leaving the room, she glanced back. She thought within herself, and could not help laughing,

"What a silly person I am! why I always wet the towels myself. What have I done? hung the dry towels over the wet ones; of course all the wet will pass through them and damp them. Surely, I have never observed properly till to-day."

Many girls think that the habit of making rational observations on what passes before them is not to be learnt; that the power of observation is a gift. But this is not true. Every body observes, just as Mary always observed that her master's towels were damp; and after she had been helped by a good mistress to use her reason a little, she observed that the fault was her own. But a girl can be a good mistress to herself. She can teach herself to observe with sense, and behave with understanding. That she should do so is often most important to those around her.

A young woman in a nursery once observed that a little boy of about six years of age shrunk when she touched his knee. "Stand still, Master Charles," she would say; "how can I dry your leg properly, if you shake like that?" or, "I can't pull your stocking up straight if you catch your knee away." This went on for some weeks, till at last the child screamed when he was touched, and the upper-nurse inquired what the matter was. Then it was found out that the boy had been sliding down the banisters of the stairs, which he knew was a forbidden play, and so, when he had fallen and hurt his knee, he had not liked to tell. "Have you observed that this knee is swelled to-night?" "I think it often looks like that," was the stupid reply. The end was, that within the year that little boy had his leg taken off; and the nurse said, "It all might have been saved, if you had observed as you ought to have observed, and reasoned as you ought to have reasoned. You have plenty of sense, and it is of no use to you— you have no observation." The girl improved very much after this; but she used to say, that the sound of the child's wooden leg almost broke her heart. Here is another instance of a want of proper observation.

There was a large old house built close to the public road. You entered from the road into a great square court, where stables and offices stood, and where the entrance-door of the house opened from a high square hall. The road was one which was much traversed both by night and by day. One morning, as early as two o'clock, when the moon was bright, a man passing by saw smoke coming from the house. "Brewing, I suppose," he said to himself; "but it is a bad time of year to brew." He was a man of no observation. Another passed by, and he too saw the smoke, which was getting thicker. "Washing, I suppose," he said to himself; "but how odd to be washing so late in the week!" And then, soon after, another man passed that way. He stopped, saw the smoke, observed that it came from the centre of the house, where no offices were likely to be; and he cried loudly, "Fire! fire!" He climbed over the door, got into the court, rang the bell, threw up small stones to the windows, and succeeded in alarming the house. Half the house was burnt down, but happily all lives were saved; the destruction of furniture, books, and pictures, was very great. If the first of these men had seen with understanding, the whole might have been saved.

Cultivate your powers of observation. Many times a day you may give yourself a lesson, and many times a day from your own observation you may gather knowledge, and thus daily grow a more valuable person in your state of life, whatever that state of life may be.

You will also make observations about other people. These observations, if you have read and remembered all that is written in this book, you will find that justice will often require you to keep to yourself; and yet that kindness may require you to mention them; and if so, good management will teach you something as to the way in which you ought to speak.

But the chief use of observation, as regards other people, is to know good company from bad; to know who to cultivate as friends, and who to avoid as the enemies of your soul; for some persons may be a pleasure and a profit to you, and others would only lead you into intemperate enjoyments, which end in sorrow and sin.

And the one great observation which is to be made on this life of ours, which God has appointed to each one of us, some leading it in one place and manner, and some in another, is this: that we are all of us called on to love and serve Him, and that we are born into this world to adorn our places in His Church, and that the true end for which our lives are given us, is to save our souls.

As you grow older and older, if you lead Christian lives, you will understand this better and better. You will observe and feel that there is nothing worth having but heaven, and that only God Himself can satisfy the soul.

Love and serve God, then, in every action of your life, and with every faculty of your soul.

CHAPTER XVI.

OBEDIENCE.

THE last afternoon had arrived. The girls had been very busy all day. The new clothes were all washed and marked and folded, ready to go into each girl's trunk; and those trunks stood on a long bench in the workroom, and Sister Angela had written the different directions and fastened them safely on.

The room was still, the blinds drawn down; for the afternoon sun was hot and glaring.

Some of the little girls had cried because these three young women, who had always been good and kind to them, were going away. These little children knew nothing of that world into which their friends were going; and there was something rather awful to their young hearts in the packing of the clothes, and in the new names of the places on the direction-cards. They even looked at the strong cord that lay on the floor as something strange, and wondered if it was possible for the girls to be lost, and never to be heard of any more. Bigger girls laughed a little at these little ones; and they showed them the map, and on it the names of the places that were written on the cards; and one or two of the girls had seen these very places, and they told of the pleasant country, the bright hedgerows, the sunny banks, where they had watched the butterflies on the primroses, and seen the young lambs at play in the fields, and gathered yellow lilies among the apple-trees in the orchards. A half-holiday had been given to these children; and when the little ones ran out to play, the elder girls welcomed Mrs. Maitland, who came in, looking very happy, to speak to her young friends for the last time in that way and in that room. They gathered round her, and placed a chair for her to sit upon.

"What have you got to do?"

"We have some pocket-handkerchiefs to mark, ma'am."

The lady took some knitting from a basket she carried in her hand, and as she began to arrange the knitting-needles she said,

"What are we to speak about to-day? What is the great crowning virtue, without which all others are imperfect?"

The girls looked up; each one spoke, and spoke truly: "Obedience, ma'am."

"Yes, obedience. Let us take for our last subject that greatest of virtues,—Obedience."

Christian obedience is not bondage; it is victory. Those who obey Satan are in bondage, but those who obey God are free.

"But," said lively little Jane Isles, suddenly interrupting Mrs. Maitland,—"but I, ma'am, shall have to obey an upper servant, a cook, and she may not be kind, and possibly she may not be good, and yet I must obey her; and surely that will be bondage and a trial; and often I have wondered, if she should be disagreeable, what I am to do."

Mrs. Maitland, with a gentle smile, said, "You must obey, dear child; you must be quick to do her will, ready to take her orders; she is your superior for the time being, and you know from whom all superiors derive their right to obedience."

"Yes, from God," said Jane; "but would an unkind, ill-behaved woman derive *her* right from God?"

"Yes; just the same as if she were kind and the best example in the world, though she may abuse her power."

"I can't understand, ma'am," said Jane.

All the girls listened eagerly to this conversation.

"This superior, whoever she may be, will have no power to make you do any thing contrary to the law of God. You obey those who are set over you *in* God, not *above* and *before* God. You understand that."

"Yes."

"If the person under whom you are to serve told you to commit any kind of sin, should you obey her?"

"No."

"If she put very hard work on you, or subjected you to unjust orders, should you obey her?"

"I don't know," said Jane.

"Yes," said Mary Hardy.

"Mary has given the right answer. You may leave any place in which you are treated with unkindness and injustice. You may plead your own cause and try to get better usage; but if you cannot get the law altered, then it is Christianlike to obey it. And while you live under that law, however disagreeable it may be to you, you will behave in a Christianlike way to obey willingly and cheerfully, silently and humbly, not complaining, and never allowing yourself to give way to inward complainings and self-pityings. Do you know what I mean?"

"Yes," said all the girls, "we know what you mean, ma'am,—not to indulge in unspoken grumblings, not to keep up a feeling of ill-usage in one's heart."

"Yes, that is exactly what I mean. To obey with a holy indifference, as if you *would not* feel, and were determined not to judge whether your treatment was good or bad, kind or unkind; such obedience is very good and brave, and just what, in difficult situations, a true Christian ought to practise."

"I can understand," said Anne Wilton, "that such obedience must be pious, but I can't understand how any one can call it victory; it seems to me to be real slavery, and nothing else."

"My dear child," said Mrs. Maitland, "there may be suffering in obedience sometimes; and before you have disciplined your heart into cheerful, humble, simple obedience; but it never is slavery, because you obey," —she stopped—" Anne, why do you obey?"

"I obey because I am a Christian."

"Explain what you mean."

"I mean," said Anne thoughtfully, "that if I were a heathen, or one who did not love God, I should not obey, I should only obey when it pleased me to obey. I should not obey any one who was unkind, or any one who told me to do what I did not like to do; but being a Christian, I know that God has appointed my place in life, and has subjected me to its trials for my discipline and purification, and so I take them as well as I can. I don't rebel, lest I should be setting myself up against God; so I obey, because I am a Christian."

"And do you call that slavery, Anne?"

"Yes, ma'am; I might do right, I might obey; but I think it would be slavery still."

"Your obedience, under such trying circumstances, would prove that you believed in God."

"Yes, ma'am."

"That you were willing to honour God by staying where He had placed you, even against your own inclinations."

"Yes, ma'am."

"And your obedience would show that you chose to trust God; and surely, if you believe, and honour and trust God, and if such belief and honour and trust combine to keep you in a difficult place, preferring its trials to the possibility of offending your dear Lord, who sees you, and watches and loves you, surely, my dear child, such obedience has a better name than slavery. Tell me, Anne, tell me that better name."

But Anne's face was red, and her eyes bright with tears.

"I know the name," she said; "it is not slavery, it is love."

"Yes, you are right; it is love. All things are easy to those who love God. And many Christians so ardently wish to give all they have to give to God, that they desire to give up their own will; they would rather not have their own way, they prefer in some way to serve. And though you are obliged to serve, my dear girls, you need not lose the merit of it. Perhaps you would rather be possessed of independent means; perhaps you would rather be the mistress than the maid. Then, give up that desire, annihilate that will; accept heartily and lovingly the position your dear Lord has chosen for you, and obey all who are placed over you for His dear sake. Every time you are tried by any want of kindness in the persons placed over you, renew this offering of your will to God. Once more, in this way, give Him your heart, who so loved you as to give you Himself. Thus, every moment of annoyance will be turned into an occasion of praise; and you turn into a glorious action what might have been a grieving pain."

"That is victory," said Anne Wilton. "Yes, obedience is the greatest of virtues, and not slavery, but homage; not bondage, but victory. I pray God I may never forget that."

"The way of obedience our Blessed Redeemer chose; and He has made the way of servitude for ever glorious. My dear young friends, make it your honour and happiness to live as He lived; to do as, in His adorable humility, He has done."

"Is there no more?" asked Jane Isles; "is there no more, dear Mrs. Maitland?"

The lady smiled very lovingly on Jane. "You

must tell all that remains to be told in the speaking actions of a good life."

And these girls did, by their good lives, give many lessons and much encouragement. You, dear readers, must be told in conclusion what the first two years did.

At the end of that time their different mistresses wrote to the convent, in whose school they had been taught; and in these letters the three girls were described as every thing that good Christian servants ought to be. When Sister Angela had heard the letters read, she went to the chapel; and kneeling before the Blessed Sacrament, thanked God. The school-girls had a half-holiday, at the request of Mrs. Maitland, and she provided tea and cake in the evening.

As Mrs. Maitland was returning home, some one touched her gown. She took no notice at first, supposing that it was an accident. But again her dress was pulled, and now looking round, she saw a girl she had known three years before, and who at that time was a friend of Mary Hardy.

"Is it Emma Morris?" asked Mrs. Maitland.

"I want to be good," sobbed forth the girl.

"May God bless my dear girl! Make a good resolution, and practise it courageously. When did you go to your duties last?"

"Three years ago."

"And you want to be good? Oh, thank God for that. Walk on by my side. Where do you live?"

"With my mother, in Fox's Alley."

"That is close by. I will go there with you."

"No, no!" said the girl.

"Why not?" asked Mrs. Maitland.

"Mother's drunk," said Emma, with a shudder.

Mrs. Maitland did not speak.

"O my dear lady," cried the girl, "don't desert me. I have done no dreadful things. I have not quite forgotten God. But it has been so hard. Poor mother takes my earnings. We are down so low I can't earn much. When I got so badly off in clothes,"—she held up her naked foot,—"I was ashamed to go to Mass. Then I left off my duties. Now my heart will break. I want to be good."

"Why do you want to be good?" asked Mrs. Maitland.

"O ma'am, I was once Mary Hardy's friend; and Jane Isles used to tell me of things said to them before they went to service. And now I have heard all the school rejoicing for their two years' good character and perseverance; and I have had two years of misery, and no one will ever rejoice over me,—yet I want to be good."

"This evening the confessional is attended by Father Francis, who is the confessor of the school-girls. Will you go and speak to him?"

"Yes," said Emma.

"I shall not take you. You must go by yourself, of your own free-will."

"I will go," said Emma.

"Can you say your prayers?"

"Some of them."

"Answer me, then, as we stand here, in a whisper."

And Mrs. Maitland and Emma Morris said the "*Hail Mary*" softly together in that crowded street. Then Mrs. Maitland went home; and Emma almost ran to the chapel. The next Sunday this girl, once a tidy school-girl, stood to hear Mass, without shoes or stockings, and with her tattered garments wrapped around her.

"Come with me," said Mrs. Maitland, "after Mass."

She went to Mrs. Maitland's house, and was there clothed decently from head to foot. She joined the adult evening class at the convent, and soon knew her religion perfectly once more, and began diligently to practise it. The priest got her a place in a small shop near the convent.

This happy return of a wandering soul may be traced to the good conduct of the three girls who had received Mrs. Maitland's instructions. And the good these girls did by their example did not end here. When Emma Morris's mother saw how steadily her daughter persevered in the practice of her religion, she began to feel the pangs of self-reproach; and by God's blessing she herself returned to the Church, from which she had for many years been an outcast.

It is certainly true, my dear readers, that we cannot any of us live to ourselves. If we sin, we injure others besides ourselves; and by the mercy of God, if we do well, we do His work, and are a help and an encouragement to weak souls who require assistance.

Hoping to spread the benefits of good example, these instructions are offered to you in a book. If you find pleasure in reading them, then pray for your fellow-labourers, and for that one who has written them for you.

THE END.

www.ingramcontent.com/pod-product-compliance
Lightning Source LLC
Chambersburg PA
CBHW020916230426
43666CB00008B/1471